A DIARY OF OVERSEAS SERVICE:

BRITISH EXPEDITIONARY FORCE FRANCE

1915-1918

DAVID WINDER SMALL

ROYAL ENGINEERS SIGNALS

The major portion of this book
comprises the words of
David Winder Small
transcribed by
Felicity Jane Laws,
one of his nieces,
as the Diary
has become her property
thus the
copyright © also.

My intention is that the original diary be lodged with the Imperial War Museum for safekeeping and access.

Dedicated to those who returned
in memory of who they were
before they went

FORWARD

David Winder Small, born 8th July 1895, joined the Signals Section, Royal Engineers and served with them in France and Flanders during the First World War, initially as a despatch rider and then as a Signals Officer until the Armistice; he was awarded the 1914-15 Star, the British War Medal 1914-18 & the Victory Medal 1914-18.

After demobilization he taught at the prestigious Haberdashers' Aske's School; he married Olivia Laws and they had one son, Roger. David served in the Home Guard during WWII and died in October 1957.

Before uncovering his exquisite handwritten diary, I knew virtually nothing about my uncle David: the text reveals a portrait of a brave but gentle person who I'm sure I would have loved; he writes with humour and insightful honesty of his part in desperate and dangerous events and was, in my opinion, one of many unsung heroes, giving their youth and innocence willingly for their belief in their country; treated a great deal less well than cattle, the brightest and the best, thousands of whom never returned to record their adventures but remain scattered in the earth of foreign lands. After the war, those who had died were fêted as heroes but many of those who returned were unable to find a place in the new world they had fought to create.

How different our world would be now had the lessons so many died to teach been learnt then, yet as I write young men and women still die daily in conflicts far from their homes. But that need not mean their sacrifice was in vain, I offer this story as a tribute to their courage and with the hope that one day the echo of their voices will be heard by those who purport to lead nations in all our names yet squander the potential of the next generation in pointless pugnacity; may there one day be a better way to settle differences.

Should anyone mentioned within these pages be known to you and you would like to supply further information I would be happy to receive this. I can supply scans by email of maps and/or notebook pages for readers with a particular interest in these items : flissoh@hotmail.com.

1915

SUMMARY OF DATES PRIOR TO EMBARKATION

Jan 20: Became instructor of French and German to 20th Divisional Royal Engineers at Inkerman Barracks, Woking, as Sergeant attached from OTC, living in Officers Mess.

Feb 24: Division moves to Godalming district and REs are split up. The Divisional Signal Company, with whom I remain, moves into billets at Shackleford. Billeted with Corporal Taylor (motorcyclist) at the house of Mr Kimler.

Mar 13: Company moves into huts at Witley Camp near Godalming. I return to Officers Mess.

1st week in April: Division moves to Salisbury Plain (Larkhill). I live with the motorcyclists and mess with the sergeants.

June 21: Having got the RE doctor to pass me fit, I enlist as motorcyclist corporal RE at Chatham, having been acting unofficially as such for the last two months.

July 20: The 20th Division proceeded overseas, this and the following days: the Headquarters and No 1 Sections of the Divisional Signal Co. proceeded from Larkhill to Southampton, the port of embarkation.

The motorcyclists, together with the Company's 10hp Singer car and the 3-ton lorry, set off at 6.30am for Southampton by road. The Douglas cycles we had had up to the beginning of the month had recently been exchanged for 4hp Triumphs (countershaft). Arrived at Southampton Docks, we had to wait about all day with nothing to do and nowhere to go (we were not allowed to go into the town) while animals and equipment were being shipped. Before the motorcycles were taken on board, all tanks had to be emptied of petrol. There being no receptacles to receive it, the stuff was run out on the quay and into the water. Our transport was the 'Manchester Importer'. The remainder of the two sections arrived during the afternoon, having come by rail from Amesbury. While we waited on the docks some of us got into conversation – I think Cambridge was the mutual subject – with a genial officer – Captain Vick – of the 11th Durham Light Infantry, the Division's Pioneer battalion. This acquaintanceship led on many future occasions to our being given tea in the mess of this battalion when waiting for a reply to some message – indeed the officers of this battalion were always very decent to the divisional DRs.

We eventually got the order to embark soon after 6 in the evening. Some of us ensconced ourselves in the bows, but the vessel did not get under way for some time after that, and the time was spent discussing the rumours and reports which were current of the previous day's transport having been torpedoed in mid-channel, etc. When we did steam out, escorted by destroyers, it was dusk, and the uncertainty of our destination (though we assumed it – correctly as it proved – to be Havre) and the novelty of it all made the scene seem a weird one. It soon got cold in the bows, as our issue 'British warms' did not cover the knees, and we made our way further aft and got some fitful sleep under the shelter of a deck-house, though the horses and mules were very restless – kicking about all the time.

July 21: We arrived at Havre about 8am – the morning grey and rather chilly. From the sea the port looked just like any French port looks when you cross the channel for your summer holiday – it was not until the vessel was berthed that khaki troops and unwonted movement became apparent. On shore we were grateful for hot coffee obtained from a buffet on the quay run by Englishwomen for the troops. One of them looked rather grand and we thought she must be at least a duchess.

The morning was spent in working at unloading, etc. It was rather refreshing to see curiously ramshackle French shunting engines again, with their full accompaniment of voluble Gauls with penny trumpets.

In the afternoon we had to make our way up to a British 'Rest Camp' (may the authorities be forgiven for the misnomer) at Harfleur. There was a YMCA hut in the camp, where we obtained welcome additions to the not too sumptuous army fare served out to us; here also were paper and envelopes and I scrawled a note home.

About 11pm we were off again, this time to the railway station at Havre. The DRs brought up the rear of our slow-moving column of men, baggage and cable-carts, and had an unpleasant time crawling along in the darkness with engines racing almost red-hot in bottom gear. Fortunately the officers soon realized the folly of this impeded progress, and on future moves the DRs went on in front, or by a different route. Entraining at the station was a wearisome proceeding and it took our united efforts to get the wagons and mules (the latter were usually the most difficult of all) on to the train.

July 22: About 3am we got aboard ourselves – the officers in compartment carriages, NCOs and men in covered trucks – those that bear the legend '*Chevaux 8, Hommes 40*'. There were only 25 in ours, but that was quite enough. A little later we started wondering where on earth we should fetch up. Rouen was passed about dawn – a beastly station, choked with filth and fumes. The day turned out bright and sunny and we sat in the open doorways of the truck, dangling our legs outside. At Abbeville a brief halt was made to water the animals – here, we were told, were the overseas HQ of the Signal Service. Later in the war most of us visited one or more times the Signal Depot there. Here and everywhere small children waved us by with shrill demands for 'souvenir – biskeet – bully beef'. We went on up the coast line to Boulonge and on through Calais. The country looked very verdant and suggested anything but war. Once a Paris express passed and we saw well-dressed civilians dining off choice fare in one of the restaurant cars belonging to the *Compagnie Internationale des Wagons-Lits*. We were all feeling particularly hungry just then, I remember.

Someone had told us that our destination would be within ear-shot of the guns, and as we dawdled up the line I kept wondering – and a good many others were thinking the same I fancy – when we should first hear them and whether it would be a fearsome and deafening din. When we eventually did come to a final stop it was 11pm, drizzling with rain, and not a sound to be heard. The spot was just outside the station of Lumbres, near St Omer (no troop train in France ever stopped actually **in** a station to my knowledge, always a slight distance one side or the other of it by way of making things a little more difficult).

There ensued the same old business of detraining and unloading, losing everything and everybody, cursing and swearing.

After a long time it was done, so far as the Signal Company was concerned and our first Signal Office in France was set up in a room of the local chateau. Three DRs had to go on night duty right away, the remainder were permitted to spend the night in a fowl-house in joint possession with the lawful owners.

Following is a list of the officers and DRs of the company at this time:

Capt. FJM Stratton	CO
Lt PW Clark	O i/c No 1 Section
Lt FA Sclater	O i/c No 2 Section (59th Infantry Brigade)
Lt AG Brace	O i/c No 3 Section (60th Infantry Brigade)
Lt EP Reynolds	O i/c No 4 Section (61st Infantry Brigade)
Lt D Hannan	HQ
CSM Charlish	
CQMS Prentice	
Sgt Drabble	
Sgt Jones	
Sgt Bentley	
Sgt Smith	Etc all HQ and No 1 Sections
Motorcyclists:	
Sgt Hippisley	i/c DRs later commissioned in RGA. (Died January 1955)
Cpl Tindall	Artificer ['tiffy]
Cpl Wells	
Cpl GM Welsford later commissioned RFC (killed in action RFC)	
Cpl J Ritchie	

Cpl SJ Smetham ('Smethers') commissioned in RNAS, then RAF permanent commission (died post-war)
Cpl AG Gripper ('Archie') became Sgt of DRs when Hippy left
Cpl F Lester
Cpl KE Tulloch ('Keith') later commissioned RFC (believed killed in action)
Cpl I Collis ('Ivor')
Cpl RF Heilgers ('Luise')
Cpl J Taylor returned to England and civil life as a medical student
Cpl H Goode commission in RFC, gained DSO etc (killed in action)
Cpl ES Crummack ('Mac') later commissioned RE
Cpl DW Small ('Tiny') later commissioned in RE Signals
Cpl L Spencer joined us at Merris Aug 1915
Cpl G Sheldon

'Smethers' later Squadron Leader RAF.

[Message on back of postcard to David's mother, Louisa Small]

Dear Mrs Small,

I am sending you this as I was unable to get any more of the last but it will be a little reminder of our short but sweet acquaintance. Tiny and myself with many others have had a furious shave so we look pretty good convicts, however I think it is wise. Our new machines are rather a failure being miles too heavy for the job, however we have to make the best of a bad job. Now we are just off somewhere as the papers say.

Ever Yours, Stanley John Smetham.

[On rear of postcard] Best Love Luise "The Saint"!!!?

Mac

E.S. Crummack, MM and a fellow officer cadet

Jimmie Ritchie & Archie Gripper

'Luise' Heilgers on right

Archie Gripper

July 23: On seeing our surroundings by daylight we found we were billeted in outhouses of a typical French small farm, with the usual large mire in the middle, surrounded by house and outbuildings on three sides. It soon became a very familiar type of residence for us. We achieved a wash at the pump, for which we were thankful, and Hippisley drew up a system of shifts for the DRs. Three were on duty in the Signal Office (Shift 1), three more stood by in the billet in case of requirement (Shift 2), three more (Shift 3) were off duty. The Sergeant and 'tiffy did not do routine duty; the other man over was supposed to clean his machine. Shift 1 went on from 8am to 12.30, Shift 2 from 12.30 to 5pm, Shift 3 from 5 to 9pm, when the first shift came on again, for all-night duty. At first the night shift had to sleep in the Signal Office with full kit on, revolvers and all, which on a stone floor was far from restful. After about a month however this rule was relaxed (it was quite unnecessary) and we were allowed to take blankets to the Signal Office and divest ourselves of equipment and tunics during the night so long as we were not required.

During the first day at Lumbres I got one run to GHQ at St Omer - this was the only time I ever went there. At the entrance to the town a British and a French sentry stopped all comers and inspected passes. My impression of the town is that its outstanding features were clean pavé streets and British Military Police in amazing quantities.

July 24: I got a run in the evening to one of our Field-Ambulances (the 60th, 61st and 62nd were attached to the Division) in a most outlandish spot very hard to find from the meagre directions I had received. However I scored in the end by their colonel asking me into the mess and giving me a good supper.

Barring pavé in the towns the roads in this district were very fair, and superior to the atrocious tracks on Salisbury Plain which we had just left.

July 26: In the evening I was sent out to one of the Brigade Sections at Wavrans to be Brigade motorcyclist. Secured a good 'bed' in a hayloft, but only stayed one night with them. A couple of days after this, July 28, the Division got orders to move, and Divisional Headquarters spent the first night of the march at Lynde. We had a hectic time trying to locate elusive units. One of my runs was to Hazebrouck.

July 29: The move continued. The DRs were allowed to go by a different route, thus enabling us to go at our own pace. We went via Steenbecque, Pont Levis and Vieux Berquin to Merris, which became Divisional HQ for about three weeks. At Vieux Berquin we saw slowly moving strings of refugees, coming I suppose from Armentières and making for the back areas and the coast, with all their furniture and belongings piled on all manner of strange vehicles. There seemed to be many men of military age among them, whom we thought would be better employed marching in the other direction.

Merris was a small village about 4 miles south west of Bailleul. The church had a few holes in the roof from German shells, and the Germans themselves had been in the village for a few days in 1914, but had soon retired. When we were there, however, it was more than 10 miles from the nearest part of the front line. HQ were in a large convent school, the NCOs of the Signal Co were billeted in a large bare room in the upper storey of an estaminet in the market square. The nights were cold, but as it was officially summer in the eyes of the army we had no blankets. We filched some canvas postal-sacks and tried to gain extra warmth by their covering, but it did not amount to much.

Our company transport was parked in a field at the other end of the village, wither we had to walk for our meals. Gripper and I and one or two others frequently supplemented these with omelette and potatoes at one of the estaminets we passed on the way. Mails from home, which had been necessarily somewhat irregular during our moves, began to arrive pretty regularly and I was very well supplied with extra food and other welcome items from Hampstead. Especially useful were the electric torches and lamps which, with refills therefor, from time to time arrived in response to my demands – they were absolutely indispensable for night work.

Our regular runs from Merris were to 3rd Corps HQ in the Hotel de Ville at Bailleul, to the three brigades at Oultersteen, Le Verrier and Ecole de Steentje (near Noote Boom) respectively and to various Divisional units at Vieux Berquin (Supply Column), Strazeele, Pradelles, etc. Before we left, the Corps HQ moved from Bailleul to the Chateau at La Motte-au-Bois, south east of Hazebrouck.

July 31: I got a run to railhead at La Gorgue (Estaires) and there saw for the first time a German plane over the town at a great height being fired at by our archies [anti aircraft guns]. Two Indian Divisions had their headquarters in this neighbourhood, the Meerut Division at La Gorgue, and the Lahore Division at Nouveau Monde, and it was a novel sight to see numbers of turbaned native troops. My messages delivered I procured an excellent beef steak and fried potatoes at a small estaminet in Estaires, fare which I had not eaten for many days.

2nd week in August: Each Brigade in turn went into the line at Armentières and Laventie for a trial experience. This was a quiet piece of the front. I was attached for a week to the Divisional Artillery HQ, but as they were at Merris also I remained in the same billet. Later I was sent as a motorcyclist to 61st Bde HQ in the school at Steentje. The brigade at the time was in the line at Armentières and Steentje was a rear headquarters. Smetham worked between forward and rear brigade, living at the forward HQ and I between rear HQ and Division. He was the first of the DRs to visit the trenches (at Armentières) and we listened with great interest to his account of looking through periscopes and firing a sniper's rifle.

Several times I got permission to go to Bailleul, where, at a house near the station one could obtain a hot bath which was a great joy. The last troops in Bailleul had been Australians. The Australian private gets 6/- a day, and prices had accordingly risen to an absurd height, which hit us hard when we wished to purchase extra luxuries.

The natives of this region spoke both French and Flemish, those of Steentje itself seemed to have a curious parlance – sounding like a cross between Scotch and Flemish – of their own. The Signal Section was billeted in one of the school rooms, whose furniture was restricted to some stacked-up wooden forms and a number of sacks of very lousy clothing. The walls were adorned with maps of the department of the Pas-de-Calais and of the Nord, and various diagrams, typically French. One was entitled *l'Empoisonnement d'Alcool*, and graphically displayed the downward path of the drunkard's career. Another was a kind of gradient profile of the rulers of France, from the Mérovingiens and Carolingiens via Capétiens and Valois to those '*de nos jours*'. I did not grasp its full significance but some of the 'gradients' appeared very precipitous.

Aug 16: Back at Divisional HQ at Merris. The duty shifts here were 7am to noon, noon to 5pm, 5pm to 10pm, 10pm to 7am. Three shifts as before. From time to time we got other jobs to do. This day for instance I was in charge of the 3-ton lorry on a trip round the brigades delivering stores. Not an arduous task – merely sitting in the front and supervising the off-loading at the various halts. The two men who have charge of this lorry, and the driver of the OC's Singer car, are ASC MT men attached to the company.

Aug 25: A sleeping bag arrived from home, which was a tremendous asset. So many parcels reach me from home and so many items do I request that I feel like the young cuckoo – the more one stuffs down its greedy gorge the more does it demand.

We were expecting to move about this time, and one of the brigades (59th) had already gone into the line, with its HQ at Laventie, a place which got shelled intermittently, though this front as a whole was a relatively very quiet one. I got a run to this Bde on the 25th and they told me they had had a dose that morning but all was quiet when I was there. The roads in this district were very different from those round Merris. They were mostly pavé and wretchedly bumpy, while in bad grease they were almost unrideable, and later in the year when the long fine summer weather had eventually given place to autumnal rains we had some very trying times. I got a run one evening to 1st Army HQ at Aire and got back quite late.

Aug 28-31: We moved on one of these days from Merris to Nouveau Monde near Estaires, where we took over Divisional HQ from the Lahore Division, in the Chateau. The Signal Office was in a roomy cellar, not much below ground level and lighted with electric light manufactured on the premises by the owner of the Chateau. (These were days before the introduction of Portable Electric Lighting sets to the equipment of Headquarters.) Headquarters section was billeted in the upper part of a large brick outhouse, which had a cement floor, very cold at nights. The flies were a beastly nuisance, they seemed to be unusually prolific and parts of the roof were completely covered with them. The cook-house was the other side of a meadow by the side of the River Lys, which through constant passage of troops, and horses going to water, soon became a sea of liquid mud almost up to the knees in some places. Gum boots became a *sine qua non* – and they were also extremely useful when using outstretched legs as outriggers in riding on greasy pavé, as the rubber slid easily over the surface, but the sole of the stoutest gum boot will not survive this usage for long.

From Nouveau Monde the regular runs were as follows:

3rd Corps	La Motte-au-Bois
The 3 Brigades	Laventie and Rouge de Bout
8th Divn	Sailly-sur-Lys
27th Divn	Croix Du Bac
Guards Divn	La Gorgue
Divl Supply Col	Vieux Berquin

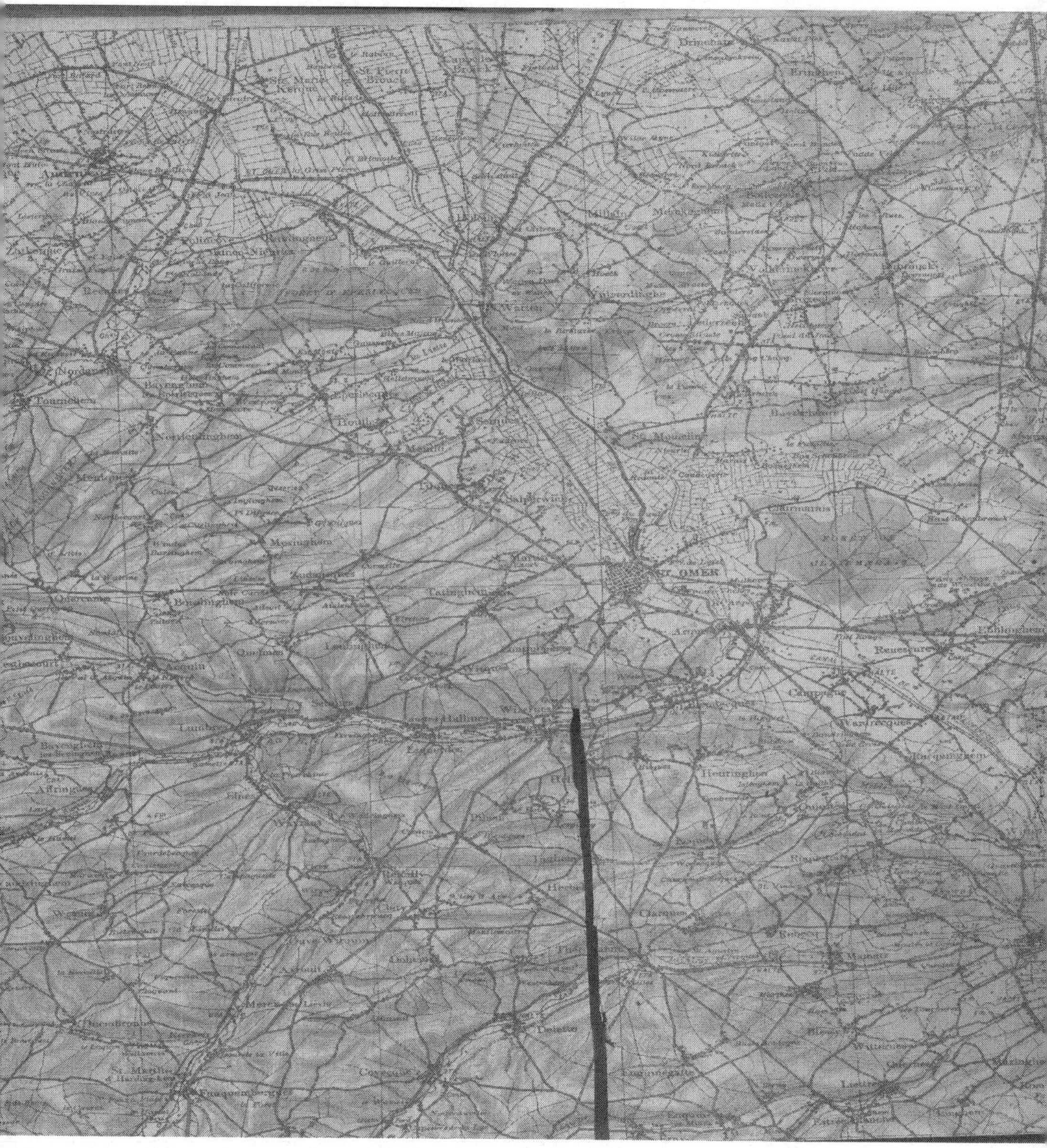
ST. OMER
Watten
Lumbres

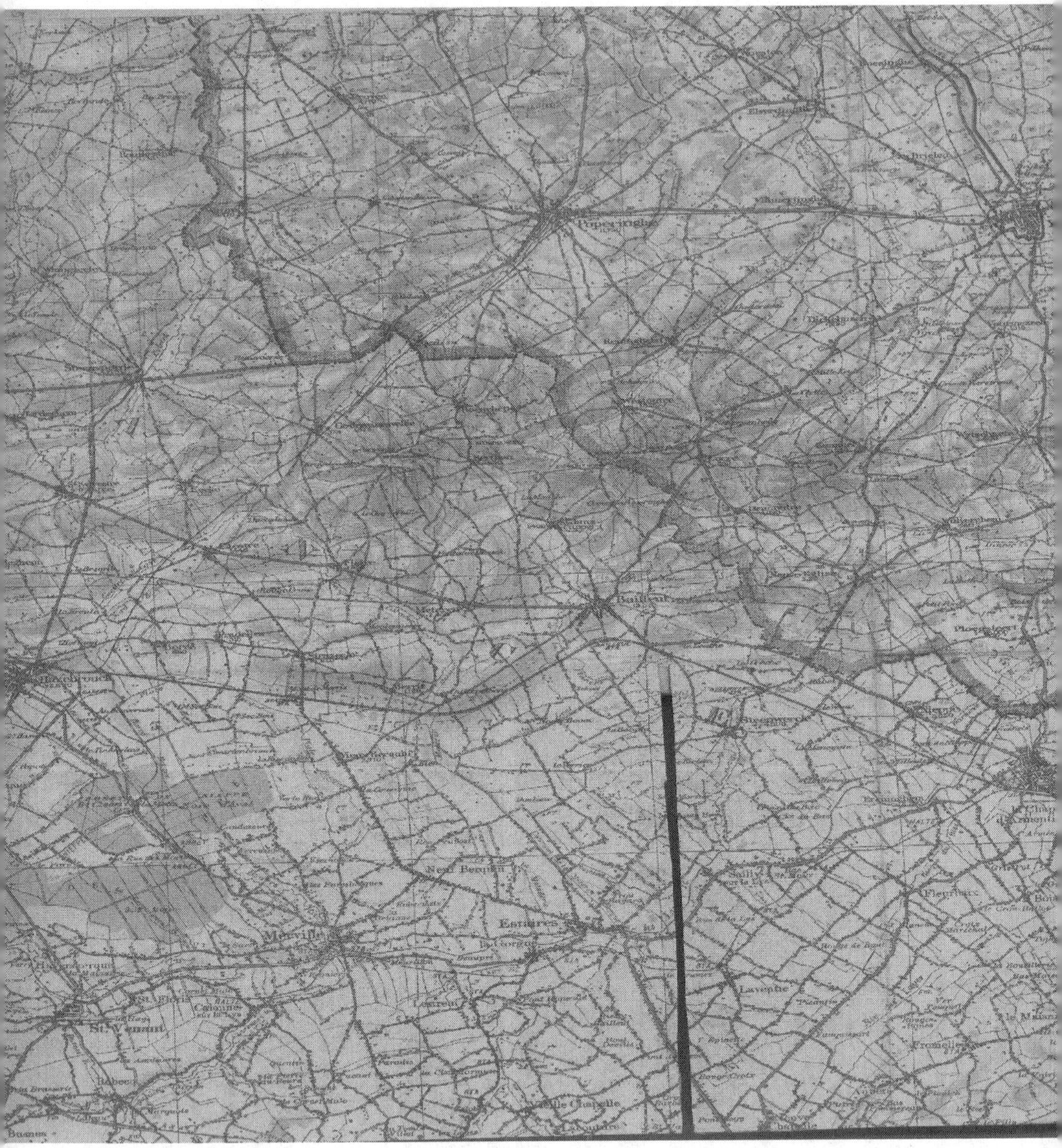

The despatches and correspondence were taken round these units at stated times during the day ('Posts'), usually three or four during the 24 hours. The runs between Corps and Divisions were made partly by us and partly by Corps DRs; those between Division and Brigades were supplemented by extra 'posts' brought by the

Divisional DR attached to each Brigade HQ (these were changed every week). Isolated units were usually run to as occasion demanded. In addition, urgent messages were taken out any time provided they were franked by a Staff Officer entitled to send 'Priority' messages. This system of posts was of course greatly superior to the haphazard way of taking out messages just when the sender or the signal clerk thought fit, irrespective of their importance or urgency, but there was still room for some grumbling (as indeed there always will be in the army, no matter how perfect the arrangements). The Divisional Orders, for example, which were issued daily, had always to be taken round all units of the division the same day. They were supposed to be issued by 5pm, but frequently did not arrive from the Headquarters Office till nearly 9. This meant scouring the country in the darkness to find all the isolated units and probably having to rouse up an officer or orderly room clerk at the other end, who having signed for their receipt very surlily, would usually cast the envelope down and think no more of it till morning. (Any really urgent orders affecting operations were invariably sent out immediately by special DR, so that it was only routine stuff that went by this evening 'post'.)

I remember one such run when orders had come in particularly late, and the night was dismally dark and wet. My run was to the Mobile Veterinary Section who were at a farm off the Vieux Berquin road. After passing Neuf Berquin I heard a tremendous roaring above the noise of my engine and my headlamp showed up some great moving mass apparently taking up the whole of the road. (We were allowed headlights rearwards of Divl HQ but not in front.) I got to the extreme side of the road, almost in the ditch, just in time to avoid these objects, which proved to be a couple of 200hp Holt caterpillar tractors, the first I had seen, wandering up without lights – no doubt to move some heavy guns further up. Arrived, about 10.30 at my destination I left my bike in the farm-yard and endeavoured to find the 'office' of the unit. My electric torch had given out and I commenced the search by falling into the farm mire. Nobody appeared to be on the premises (the section, I afterwards found, slept in an outhouse some little way from the farm) – at length however, I succeeded in rousing someone in a room at the back, who proved to be the Officer commanding the unit. Very sleepily he lit a candle, signed my receipt and opened the envelope.

Inside was a large sheet of foolscap headed in typewritten letters '20th Divisional Routine Orders by the Major General…etc, commanding' and the date and signed at the bottom by a staff major. The remainder of the sheet was blank except for the word 'Nil' neatly typewritten somewhere about the middle. The Commanding Officer's language and my feelings are better left to the imagination!

Sept 4: I was attached to 61st Bde HQ in Estaires prior to their moving into the line. This they did the next day, and Bde HQ were established (Sept 5) in a farmhouse at Rouge de Bout. The Signal Office was in a barn, with the lines duplicated into an adjacent dug-out in case of emergency. I established myself in this dug-out together with Curtis, one of the Brigade Section NCOs. The runs from Bde to Divn averaged four a day each way.

Sept 7: A scarcity of orderlies at Bde HQ so I took out some messages for the battalions in the line and thus paid my first visit to the trenches. The communication trenches were very muddy though the weather had been fine. There was a fair amount of artillery fire on both sides, but in the trenches everyone save sentries, snipers and machine gunners seems to sleep, waking up at night and starting up rifle and MG fire to the accompaniment of flares and Very lights. This was of course then one of the quietest parts of the line.

Sept 9: Bde HQ shelled with whizzbangs [high speed shells] and shrapnel, commencing 7am and lashing intermittently throughout the day. Two cottages on the opposite side of the road were fired and burned down, but the only casualty was one civilian wounded. The signal office was transferred to the dug-out, and later in the day HQ were moved to another farm further along the road, which had previously been the HQ of the battalion in reserve. I was in demand all day, and only got many punctures for my labours. However at midnight, at the HQ of the 7th Somerset Light Infy, their Signal Officer Duff-Stevens, a Trinity man and ex-DR, gave me some very welcome food and drink in their mess.

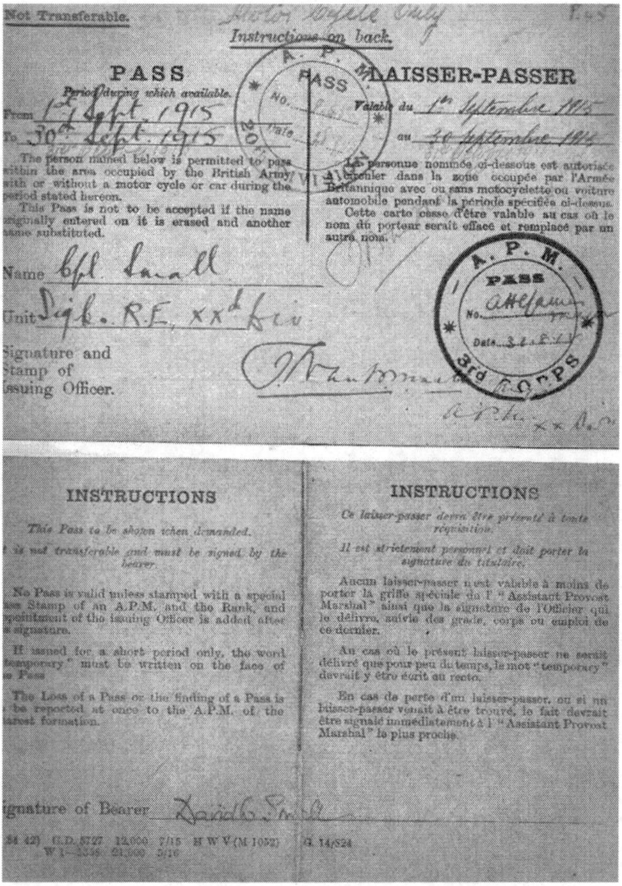
Not Transferable.

Instructions on back.

PASS

Period during which available.

From 1st Sept. 1915

To 30th Sept. 1915

The person named below is permitted to pass within the area occupied by the British Army with or without a motor cycle or car during the period stated hereon.

This Pass is not to be accepted if the name originally entered on it is erased and another name substituted.

LAISSER-PASSER

Valable du 1er Septembre 1915

au 30 Septembre 1915

La personne nommée ci-dessous est autorisée à circuler dans la zone occupée par l'Armée Britannique avec ou sans motocyclette ou voiture automobile pendant la période spécifiée ci-dessus.

Cette carte cesse d'être valable au cas où le nom du porteur serait effacé et remplacé par un autre nom.

Name

Unit

Signature and Stamp of Issuing Officer.

A. P. M. PASS No. Date 3rd CORPS

INSTRUCTIONS

This Pass to be shown when demanded.

[illegible] is not transferable and must be signed by the bearer.

No Pass is valid unless stamped with a special [illegible] Stamp of an A.P.M. and the Rank, and [illegible]ointment of the issuing Officer is added after [illegible] signature.

If issued for a short period only, the word "temporary" must be written on the face of [illegible] Pass.

The Loss of a Pass or the finding of a Pass is [illegible] be reported at once to the A.P.M. of the [illegible]arest formation.

INSTRUCTIONS

Ce laisser-passer devra être présenté à toute réquisition.

Il est strictement personnel et doit porter la signature du titulaire.

Aucun laisser-passer n'est valable à moins de porter la griffe spéciale de l' "Assistant Provost Marshal" ainsi que la signature de l'Officier qui le délivre, suivie des grade, corps ou emploi de ce dernier.

Au cas où le présent laisser-passer ne serait délivré que pour peu de temps, le mot "temporary" devrait y être écrit au recto.

En cas de perte d'un laisser-passer, ou si un laisser-passer venait à être trouvé, le fait devrait être signalé immédiatement à l' "Assistant Provost Marshal" le plus proche.

Signature of Bearer

Sept 10: Succeeded at the Bde by Smetham and I returned to the Division at Nouveau Monde. During the next week three DRs from the Westmoreland and Cumberland Yeomanry (who were our Divisional Mounted Troops) were attached to us – their overseas establishment not permitting of their retention. They were all good fellows – Hedley, Rutherford and Brown. Being thus 3 DRs to the good, three of us (myself one of them) were put onto the job of Signal Clerk in the Signal Office. This consisted in entering up in a book all messages – whether telegrams or despatches – that came in, sending out the wires by orderlies to their addresses at Divl HQ or giving them to another telegraphist to re-send if they were for a distant unit, and despatching the motorcyclists' 'posts' and 'specials'.

The Signal Office was in charge of a Senior NCO known as the 'Superintendent', a job demanding calmness and much tact. Later on I and one or two other DRs got put on to this job also, but our lack of technical knowledge often got us into difficulties and sometimes into hot water.

Several of the DRs had lately instituted an unofficial mess at a cottage near by, where for a small charge the Madame cooked our rations for us and added vegetables, etc from her garden. This was a welcome change.

From the week beginning Sept 13 I was in the Signal Office for nearly three weeks, and consequently was doing this 'cushy' if somewhat tiring job all throughout the period when the battle of Loos and subsequent fighting were going on. As the DRs had a particularly sticky time during this I was not over-pleased at this state of affairs, as it meant telling others to take out messages on what must have been very objectionable runs while I was snug and dry in the office. However, since all the messages coming through the office pass through the Signal Clerk's hands (amounting to from four to six hundred a day) I was able to get a good idea of how things were going on. To be even Signal Clerk during this period was no sinecure, and meant working 'all out' as long as one was on duty.

Sept 25: The objective of 20th Division at the time of the battle of Loos was Auber's Ridge – one of the Rifle Brigade battalions reached the German third line, but later, finding themselves cut off, were compelled to retire.

Sept 26: Brown, one of the DRs attached from the Yeomanry, was laid up with a painful internal ailment which the MO failed to diagnose. It became worse and he was sent home; it proved later to be poisoning from gas-shells encountered on a journey to 61st Brigade. He told us he had lain for two hours in a small shelter while the Boche shelled a crossroads which lay in front of him on his route.

Oct 1: The fighting has fizzled out and I went out as DR to the 61st Bde at Rouge de Bout. During the past week the brigades had moved their staffs to battle headquarters nearer the line, but these had now come back to their former sites. The barn which formed our sleeping quarters was thoroughly draughty and ratty, but the section was full of cheery good fellows who always made the best of things. Edibles and volumes of W J Locke's works from home made life quite tolerable. Washing facilities were exceedingly meagre, but that doesn't trouble the private soldier over-much provided he can get a shave. This is done in an empty cigarette tin full of water which has been used for a similar purpose by scores before him. Periodically we would get a 'baths parade' to either Estaires or Sailly. The baths at the latter place were merely an array of tubs in a shed, but at Estaires some large tanks in a former salt factory had been converted into hot baths, almost large enough to swim in. And at either place clean underlinen was obtainable, for which we were always thankful as the washing and mending of clothes was not a thing for which the average man had either the time or ability. It was at Nouveau Monde that we first made the acquaintance of the genus louse, who thenceforward, but most especially in the Salient, became our inseparable ally.

Oct 9: I returned to Division and had a wash. The following week I spent as Divisional DR, and after that again did duty in the Signal Office. The 10th and 11th were spent in the 'tiffy's' shed working on my machine which had lately been running very unsatisfactorily, but the main difficulty was lack of spare parts, especially cores.

Oct 18: Estaires is a frequent resort of ours when we are off duty and we frequently supplement our rations with stuff obtained from the shops there. This day we invested in some French canned goods with the most horrible consequences to our insides. In my case it was supplemented by toothache, which had bothered me for some time.

Oct 19: I went to the Dental Ward at Merville Hospital (British) in a Siddeley-Deasy ambulance and there renounced two teeth, for which afterwards I was very thankful.

Oct 24: The weather, which hitherto had been pretty constantly fine for a long time, turned to wet and we got some awful roads. It is when the rain has ceased and the pavé commences to dry that it is at its worst. This day I took nearly 2.5 hours to do the Brigade post of 9 miles, spending whole minutes at a time in places turning helplessly round and round on the pavé. Fortunately there was a bit of a moon.

Parcels of food from home and from other kind folk greatly added to the interest of our leisure hours. My letters home were constantly full of requests for all manner of items, many of which I'm sure I could really have done without – as many had to do – but their arrival was always a great joy.

Oct 28: Welsford and Percy Jones, one of the office sergeants, went off souvenir-hunting south of Laventie and the latter got hit in the ankle with shrapnel. We learned later that he was 17 months in hospital owing to complications in the foot. We were very sorry to lose him from the company as he was a very nice fellow and a good NCO. Welsford got badly hauled over the coals by the CO for taking him off on such a jaunt. I was put into the office as Superintendent in his stead.

Oct 31: My turn for Brigade duty came round again, and I departed for the 61st Bde, who were in the same place as before. Leave for the division had started recently and everybody accordingly built great castles in the air. But as the allotment of the Signal Company was only 2 or 3 each week, brigade sections included, with preference to married and senior men, the chances for the majority of the DRs for an early departure were not high. Much of my leisure time while at the Brigade was spent in reading W J Locke, with whom I was kept well supplied from home. His books have an originality and piquancy that I found very refreshing and my opinions in this respect were shared by Smetham, to whom I passed them on, if indeed he had not managed to read my copy first while I was not there.

Nov 6: I returned to Division and the following day resumed duty as Superintendent in the Signal Office. We were suffering about this time from a spy scare – voices speaking in strange tongues had been overheard on some of the telephone circuits and for some time somebody or other was set to listen continuously for these voices. So soon as ever anything out of the ordinary was heard, however and someone in authority had been fetched, they invariably ceased. Once the OC and one of the DRs followed up the whole route of one line at night, armed with revolvers, but encountered nothing save rats. I don't think the matter was ever properly solved; it might have been induction from some circuit on which Indian native linemen were speaking, as the Indian troops were in our vicinity for some time. Once a tall swarthy individual in a turban stalked into the Signal Office with a field telephone when I was on duty and jabbered something totally incomprehensible. I was at a loss as even the Tommy's Anglo-French jargon seemed to be lost upon him. However, I showed him the line to the Indian Division on the switchboard and this seemed to satisfy him, for having rung furiously and spoken strange words to someone at the other end, he stalked away again.

At the end of this week my lack of technical knowledge brought me before the OC to explain a delay that had occurred on one of the circuits the previous night; the same lack of knowledge made the explanation difficult, and the following week I found, somewhat to my relief (Nov 14) that I was back on motorcycling duties.

12th November 1915

SCENES FROM ANOTHER LAND

I

A disused granary, top storey. Round the walls several men's beds. Some consist of straw-filled sacks, some in crude articles made out of a few logs supported on empty petrol tins. In the middle a table with a red tablecloth. Various DRs playing at chess, draughts, halma or other weirdities, apparently from someone in England. They have obtained two electric light bulbs, tapped in on a main which runs on the roof of the building and have thus a cheerful light. Enter foreman of the Mayor of …., who owns the small château.

FOREMAN: *No light electrique (speechless indignation of DRs)*

DR: *(tentatively) Pour the devil quoi?*

FOREMAN: *No light electrique (exit)*

(Loud and long assertions on the character of the foreman)

Enter an RE Corporal

RE CORPORAL: *OC says I've to cut your electric light wire. The old lad's apparently complained his dynamo's not strong enough.*

CHORUS OF DRs: *Two extra lamps make such a difference don't they?*

(Exit Cpl of REs)

Enter Mayor of…. plus bodyguard. Assisted by latter, climbs on table and attempts to extract bulb.

INDIGNANT DRs: *Here, what the hell….? Tiny (nickname for DWS), stop him for goodness sake.*

(Thus adjured, one of the DRs rises from an obscure corner and tapping the struggling man in a Gallic manner, nearly toppling him over, speaks)

DR: *Ces lampes-ci ne sont pas à vous, Monsieur.*

(Monsieur descends with lamp and prepares to exit)

DR : *M'avez-vous entendu Monsieur?*

MONS: *Oui, mais la lumière est la mienne.*

DR : *Sans doute, mais nous pouvons payer pour ça, si vous voulez (the latter with sarcasm)*

MONS: *Ah, non, c'est la dynamo. Elle ne peut pas…*

CHORUS OF DRs: *Ask him how the **** a dynamo that can drive a 50 volt motor konks out for 2 extra lamps.*

DR: *(to Monsieur, also with sarcasm) Ah, c'est donc la dynamo?*

MONS : *Oui, et s'il y a aucune lumière ici ce soir, il n'y en aura plus pour le quartier général.*

DR : *Eh, bien M'sieur. Ne vous incommodez pas. On a déjà coupé la fil. Voyez !*

(Exit Mons discomfited and minus bulbs but DRs have to read and write by candles now)

Enter Orderly Cpl with 2 men bearing post sacks, commence sorting.

ORDERLY CPL: *Corporal Small.*

CPL S: *(indifferently)* Hallo.

ORDERLY CPL: *Letter for you.*

CPL S: *(cheerily)* Bon! *(Proceeds to read same with avidity)*

ANOTHER DR: *Any for me?*

ORDERLY CPL: *No luck.*

Curtain descends to the accompaniment of hells, damns, devils and other expressions of delight.

II

A small French boutique which displays the notice GOOD CAFÉ, MILK, EGGS, BIER. *10.30AM. In the back room a middle-aged woman is cooking eggs and potatoes for 2 DRs who sit smoking Dills (Dills best cut plug is a favourite smoke of Corp DWS). As she cooks the woman relates of the advent the previous evening at 7.58pm of a French gendarme who had found soldiers eating and drinking beer. She fears a visit from the chef des gendarmes to reprimand. Enter an artillery officer in the shop and presently into back room, clamouring for a glass of beer.*

OFFICER: *Beer, Madame?*

MDME: Il n'est pas encore onze heures, monsieur. C'est défendu de vendre la bière à cette heure, vous savez ?

OFF: But beer madame ? Bon beer ?

MDME: No compris.

OFF: (seeing her glances at the clock) to DR: What is the rule here then, about this?

DR: No beer is allowed to be sold except 11 to 1 and 6 to 8.

OFF: (to Madame) But moi officier Madame, officier beer any time.

MDME: No compris.

OFF (very thirsty and desperate) to DR: Do you know any French?

DR: (casually) Oh, yes Sir.

Madame Monsieur l'officier à un très grand désir à goûter votre bière. Est-ce que vous voulez lui donner à boire, ou lui dirai je que ça ne peut pas ?

MDME : Ah, il est officier ?

DR: Oui.

MDME: Ah (doubtfully) Je ne sais pas si…..

DR: (to officer) She says she can't possibly give you a beer at this hour of the morning as that would mean the total suspension of her licence by the police, who are watching outside to see if anyone enters, sir.

OFF: Oh, I don't want to get her into trouble (Exit, still very thirsty)

The DRs eat. Enter to shop voice demanding Madame, she complies and there follows a fluent argument in the vernacular on the incident of the previous evening. Madame's part is forte, crescendo and accelerando, ending up fortissimo and prestissimo.

VOICE :….. eh bien, trois jours. Aujourd'hui douze, ça fait le quinze, n'est ce pas ?

MDME: (fortissy-prestissywissimo) Je..je…je …vous dis….

Exit voice.

Re-enter Madame, rougissante et en grand colère.

MDME: Sale bête. Et il mangeait deux minutes, sale bête.

The DRs continue to eat after a few well-chosen words of sympathy.

MDME: (intermittently) Sale bête.

Enter several other landladies whose estaminets have been closed for longer periods on a similar charge. Gesticulations and rant. Madame begins to see the humour of the situation.

DRs: (departing) Au revoir au quinze madame.

(Madame se met à rire)

III

A signal office – on one side morse operators at their instruments, at the end a telephone operator at the exchange. On the other side the register keeper at a table on which are files of message forms, white, pink & yellow.

Foot and cycle orderlies and motor cyclists. In the middle a small table labelled 'Superintendent'. The sergeant major is in the office at work on telephone wires. The present superintendent (DWS) is a motor cyclist despatch rider who being considered to look more or less intelligent has been temporarily transferred to this post. Of dealing with messages he knows a certain amount having previously acted in the capacity of register keeper. Of the technical side of the signal office he knows next to nothing.

SUPT (to register keeper): Have you got the 5 o'clock Brigade post out yet?

RK : Yes, it's gone.

SUPT: Here are two 'special despatch rider' messages. They'll have to go now. Cpl … is the next motorcyclist. Enter them up and docket them and I'll advise by wire.

(This is done.)

TELEPH OPERATOR: Superintendent, you're wanted by xxth Corps.

SUPT (goes to phone): Hallo… Hallo…. Hell..o, who's that please?

Signal master xxth Corps? Speak up please sir, you're rather faint… yes, sir. Just a minute sir (to Sergeant Major) Here Major you might speak here will you xxth Corps want us to dis their Morse buzzer line and all sorts of things I know nothing about whatever.

(Sgt Major speaks at phone.)

Enter Orderly Sgt

ORD. SGT: Skipper wants to see you Corporal.

……

Scene changes to Signalmaster's office. OC and the senior sub to whom enter Superintendent.

OC: I've a message from the xxth Brigade and they say that at 1.30 last night the xxst Brigade asked them to call us up, as they couldn't get us. The xxth Brigade couldn't get us on either Morse circuit but eventually got through via the Artillery Exchange on the Bell telephone. Normal communication was restored at 2.10. You were on duty last night, can you give an explanation?

SUPT: Well, apparently what happened, sir, was that when you brought down a message for each Brigade last night the instruments were bunched for the night. 2nd Cpl …. said he'd send the xxst Bde one and put that instrument on its own set. Then when he re-bunched he put the plug on the commutator into a dead hole.

OC: But that would only dis the buzzer circuit. What about the sounder set? You can't put that on the Morse bunch.

SUPT feebly acknowledges want of sufficient knowledge to go any further and suggests that a clear technical account could be got from one of the telegraphists who had then been on duty. He points out that a message had been sent to the xxst Bde at 1.38am, which would naturally mean not calling up for another ¼ hour and that they called up on the telephone at 2, thus leaving only about 5 minutes to be accounted for.

OC says he will see telegraphists and SUPT hears no further development.

Exit SUPT mopping brow and returning to the office notes with relief that he is on motor cyclist duties for the next week.

Nov 22: During this week our division took over from the division on the left flank (8th Div) and Div HQ moved to Sailly-Sur-Lys, a small village a few kilometres further up the road to Armentières. During this period only two brigades were in the line at a time, the third being in reserve at Sailly. The pavé roads here were exceedingly bad. The DRs were billeted in a small house in the village, where we had our rations cooked by the woman to whom the house belonged, who was living with her relations next door.

The regular runs from here were to:

3rd Corps	La Motte-au-Bois
Left Brigade	Fleurbaix
Right Brigade	on Fleurbaix – Rouge de Bout road
23rd Division	Croix du Bac
Supply Column	Neuf Berquin
Various Divisional Units at	Estaires and Bac St Maur
181 Tunnelling Company RE	on Sailly – Rouge de Bout road
Units at	Doulieu

An order had recently come out sanctioning the release of students of medicine in their third year to return home and continue their training, owing to a growing dearth of doctors. This led to one of our number, Taylor, who was reading medicine at Birmingham, bidding us good-bye and departing, envied by us all, for Blighty. He was then with the 61st Bde. which was at that time (Nov 24) our right brigade, and I was sent there to succeed him.

More than one change had taken place among the DRs lately. Wells had left us at Nouveau Monde to take up a motor-cycling commission, Lester went to 11th Corps at Merville as a DR for duty with the carrier-pigeon service (we often marvelled at these men when we saw them ploughing their bikes through greasy pavé with a huge basket of pigeons on their backs); finally Luise skidded under a GS wagon at Sailly and departed for the base with a fractured arm. One of the reinforcements consequent on these vacancies was Bob Robson – happy-go-lucky Northcountryman who in the later years of the war was to earn the Military Medal, and was one of the few early DRs to finish up the war with the company.

Even now some of us talked vaguely of getting a commission and going off – we did not like to see the originals departing and some of their successors, however reliable as motor-cyclists, were not quite the same type of folk as the first. The 'commission-fever' flame was fanned by the officers of the 197 Land Drainage Co RE, an isolated unit miles from nowhere which was one of our 'casual' runs. We used to deliver their correspondence at the officers' mess instead of, as with most units of this sort, at the Orderly room, and were always given a cheery greeting and some food in their mess. I remember their CO frequently said to some of us that it was time we took commissions, and indeed offered to do what he could for us in that direction.

The roads to the north of this unit, round about Doulieu, were frequently flooded axle-deep, which caused us a lot of trouble and we used to wish that the energies of our Land Drainage Company acquaintances could be turned in that direction.

To return to my going out to Brigade – I found that Taylor had got permission from Reynolds, Signal Officer of the 61st to have a billet at his own expense in a cottage on the opposite side of the road – I followed suit upon my arrival and secured a feather-bed, which was a terrific luxury. Marshall and Curtis, two of the Brigade NCOs slept on mattresses on the floor of the same room. Owing to a temporary shortage of DRs, I had to do duty for both this and the left brigade in Fleurbaix, which meant a considerable amount of extra work.

Dec 9th saw me back at Division, again doing Signal clerk's duty, after a week of which I returned to ordinary divisional DR. The main Armentières road was at this time still a fine avenue of trees and I remember when on night duty soon after our arrival at Sailly, before all the leaves had fallen, being struck with the beauty of it in the early dawn. Although only about 4 miles behind the line it was never shelled, though of course the never-ceasing traffic rendered it very bad so far as surface was concerned. When, later, in the Salient we saw little but mud-colour and shell-scarred tree trunks I remembered the contrast with some regret. Our time at Sailly was in fact, so far as the DRs were concerned, rather a monotonous one; our duties were purely routine work and we saw little of the harder side of war, we had plenty of food and lived in comparative comfort, but interest was lacking. The weather was bad and the weekly cleaning of our machines became a very cold and arduous task. Nearly all our bicycles, too, were suffering from the lack of spare parts, which became acute at this time.

Dec 10: There arrived from home two large Christmas parcels which were the precursors of a series which came along from day to day containing all manner of luxuries, edible and otherwise and went far to making our Christmas, when it arrived, a most joyful festival. Among the items were an accordion and a tin whistle. No one unfortunately appeared to be master of the former, but a sergeant-major of the ASC, who was a frequent visitor to our mess, played extremely well on the whistle.

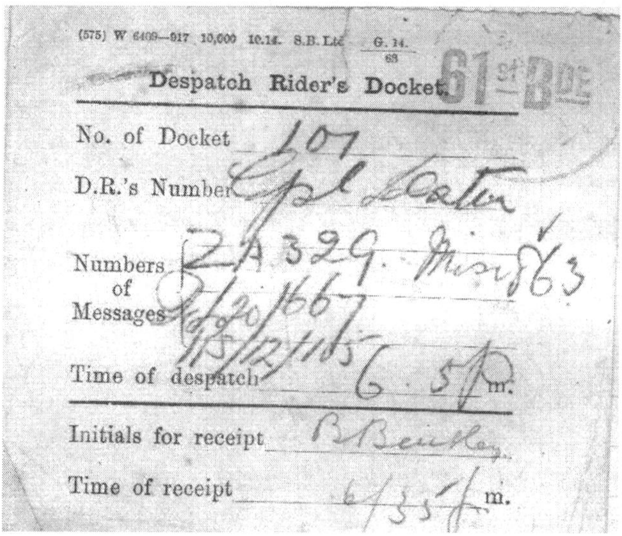

(575) W 6409—917 10,000 10.14. S.B. Ltd. G. 14. 63

Despatch Rider's Docket. 61st BDE

No. of Docket 107

D.R.'s Number Cpl Slater

Numbers of Messages ZA 329. Misc 863

Time of despatch 6.5 pm.

Initials for receipt B Bentley

Time of receipt 6/35 pm.

Dec 22: Reports of the division going out of the line for a rest in the near future, and this day I, being next for duty, was called into 'G' office and there given a map of the rest area which I was to take to 8th Div HQ (who had gone thither when we succeeded them in this sector) to get it marked into billeting and manoeuvre areas, etc for the future use of our Division. There was snow on the ground but the weather was fine when I started out about midday and I reached my destination, Blaringhem, by way of Merville, Haverskerque and Thiennes. I had to wait more than 3 hours before the map was ready to take back and whiled away some of the time with some cheery Corps who had previously been with our Division. (The Division end, as well as the Corps end, of the telegraph circuits between Corps and Divisions, were worked by Corps telegraphists, who came from

Corps HQ and lived at Divisional HQ for this purpose. In the same way, Division sent operators to the headquarters of its brigades to work the Division-Brigade circuits. They, like the DRs attached to the Brigades, were relieved at periods varying from a week to a month, though in some divisions the same DR remained with brigade permanently.)

When the time came for these telegraphists (or rather the one I knew best) to go on duty, I paid a visit to the DRs of this division, several of whom I knew slightly, and as it was then growing dark and I was not too certain of re-finding easily the rather devious route by which I had come, I accepted the offer of one of their number, who was taking their evening 'post' to Corps at La Motte via Hazebrouck, to show me the way back by the latter place. By the time I had eventually been given back the map and we had set off, it was raining hard, which made the roads very slippery. My guide, riding a light 2¾hp Douglas and knowing the route well, set off at a good 25 miles an hour and I found difficulty on the heavier Triumph in keeping up with him, as the road was full of sharp turns and my headlight burning very badly. I did not want to have to stop to remedy the latter for fear of losing him altogether.

Eventually the beam of his light ahead disappeared and I could just distinguish a T-road immediately ahead – tried to turn into it, more to save myself from running into the ditch than with any knowledge of which way I ought to go, and came a beautiful cropper on to the ground. My guide I saw no more. It was so dark that I had to feel for my bike, the last gleam of the lamp having finally given out in the upset. To my utter disgust my matches were too sodden with rain to light and there wasn't a soul about from whom to inquire the way. My back tyre, I found, was flat, but the engine I managed to start, though it would only run at a violent speed and very wheezily – the throttle control being apparently broken. I pumped up the tyre and rode as fast as I could along the road to the right (chosen at random) and fortunately passed someone who told me it led to Hazebrouck. I managed to get to the town and mended the tyre in the light of a shop window and succeeded in lighting up again. I resumed my journey only to get a burst some 4 miles further on, doubtless owing to my having carelessly nipped the tube when replacing it at Hazebrouck. It was raining so hard that the patch absolutely refused to stick, and the carbide in my generator being practically exhausted, my lamp was again dwindling. A DR then passed whom I had seen and directed on his way earlier in the day and he magnanimously took me on his carrier to his headquarters some 1½ miles down the road and there loaned me a spare tube, a most generous act considering their scarcity at that time and the uncertainty he must have had as to whether he would see it again. I tramped wearily back, but full of satisfaction, to my bike which I had left by the roadside and was further cheered by the rain ceasing. It was after 11pm when I eventually got back and I found the CO on the point of telephoning to the Field Ambulances of the neighbourhood to discover whether I had been delivered to any of them as a casualty.

Dec 23: As we were contemplating considerable festivities on Christmas Day it was decided that the fairest way of deciding who should be the Brigade DRs over Christmas was to draw lots. This was done and one of the two proved to be myself. My disgust was I fear ill-concealed as I had only recently returned from a spell of Brigade work and had been greatly looking forward to our Christmas dinner. As it turned out, however I had no possible ground for annoyance, as not only did the Brigade Signal Officer allow me to come to division for dinner but I returned after it in time for the Brigade section's festivities which were held in the evening!

Accordingly I went off to 61st Brigade at Fleurbaix and obtained sanction to billet myself in a small house opposite the Headquarters, where lived a woman with a prodigious progeny of small children, whose idea of the '*caporal anglais*' appeared to be that he existed solely to provide them with chocolate. I think their ages were fortunately too tender for them fully to realise the grimness of their surroundings. Madame was very hospitable and the bed I got there a great delight.

Dec 24: After the day's work I retired to my bed and there enjoyed opening at leisure letters and packages from home marked 'For Xmas Day' which had arrived for me. Not knowing how much leisure I should get on Christmas Day itself I thought this seemed a propitious moment to investigate their contents. The German artillery in this sector had been very inactive for a long time and Fleurbaix, though a brigade headquarters and not much more than a mile and a half from the front line as the crow flies, had been immune from shelling, though our guns had been by no means silent.

Dec 25: At 1.30 on Christmas morning however, I was woken up by shrapnel coming over into the village, either retaliation for what we had sent over earlier in the evening or perhaps just a courteous *Weihnachtsgruß*. Anyway, poor Madame was very upset and indeed most people listen to attentions of this sort with less equanimity when in a first floor bedroom than when ensconced below ground, even though one's shelter in the latter case be no more than splinter-proof. I told her I would go and find out how long it was likely to last and went across to the Signal Office where I found the night shift devouring tea and bread and cheese, in which I joined them. At 2 the shelling slacked off, so I returned and told my hostess that it was all over. Fortunately for my reputation as a kind of omnipotent comptroller of such goings-on, my assurance proved to be correct. As a matter of fact nothing had come within 150 yards of where we were.

At 9am, 10.30am and 3.30pm on Christmas Day I made my regular journeys up to Division, and, as already stated, received permission to remain there after the afternoon run for the DRs Christmas Dinner, the Brigade Sergeant undertaking to telephone for me should I be required. The feast was really a magnificent affair. For a week or so previously the DRs who went with the post to Corps (which entailed a half-hour's wait at La Motte) had made a point of filling up the interval by going on into Hazebrouck and purchasing a bottle of wine or liqueur from an excellent wine-shop there was there. The new large-sized leather despatch cases which had recently been dished out to us just contained comfortable room for the return post from Corps when one of these bottles had been deposited in the bottom. By Christmas Day, therefore, our 'cellar' contained plenty for the whole crowd of us, and by dint of diligent purchasing of provisions in various villages and small towns which our runs took us to, and by the cajoling of the good woman to borrow table cloth, plates and cutlery from half the village of Sailly, and to cook the provisions, and with the further very valuable aid of our parcels from home, we sat down, when the time came, to a right royal meal. Prior to the repast the OC came in and opened the special ration of Army rum which had been issued for the occasion (which has to be done in the presence of an officer). Healths were drunk and the Skipper made a few suitable remarks and hoped that next year would see us spending Christmas in Berlin, and then went away to do the same for one of the other messes. We then put the Army rum aside in favour of our choicer liquors (which had been carefully concealed during the opening ceremony) and settled down to enjoy ourselves. This was our menu:

Potage au riz

-

Poulets rotis
Petits pois. Sauce piquante

-

Various canned Galantines and Pâtés

-

Plum Pudding (au rhum en flammes)

-

Pêche Melba

-

Fruit. Chocolates
Cigars. Coffee

-

At the end of this terrific repast we drank sundry toasts (including that of the folk at home), and the company then abandoned themselves to cracker-pulling (the crackers had come in one of my parcels), songs and recitations. Even the serious Hippisley sang a song. Like all other good things, the feast eventually came to an end, and Ritchie (who had also got permission to come up from the other Brigade for the dinner) and myself returned to our brigades.

The week that followed was a pretty busy one. I was still (Dec 31) with the brigade at the New Year and the Boche repeated his attentions of the week before and shelled the Old Year out and the New Year in. As on the previous occasion it only lasted about half-an-hour.

1916

Thus ended the year 1915 and with it our first five months of active service. Though we were constantly grousing, it had been spent in as quiet a part of the line as one would be likely to get anywhere. The riding itself, especially when the pavé was bad, was often difficult, and so far as the ever-present liability of skids, collisions and other accidents was concerned, not a little dangerous; moreover, riding on moonless nights without a light was a very trying business – but of real war we had up to then seen little and could still easily remember the number of times we had come under shell-fire. And at that time the nightly air-raids, bane of rest-billet and back-area residence later in the war, had not yet begun to trouble us. Most of the Boche's activities in this direction were occupied with the zeppelin raids on England. If a zeppelin were seen crossing the front line anywhere in the divisional sector, the word 'zeppelin' together with the approximate location of its crossing were immediately telegraphed (or 'phoned) to Div HQ, where it was our duty immediately to circulate the news to all units. The same procedure was adopted in the case of gas alarms.

For this purpose pads of message-forms known as Gas and Zep pads were kept in the Signal office, ready addressed to all the units to which such messages, when they came, had to be sent. It was then only necessary, if a Gas or Zep alarm came through, to add the map-reference and date and hour before sending them out, which enabled this to be done more expeditiously.

It was during our occupation of this sector that the Division launched its first gas attack (night of 8-9 Jan) which proved, from all accounts, to be a rank failure. It sounded easy – take up cylinders of gas to the trenches, wait for a favourable wind, let off the gas with artillery accompaniment and then make an assault on the German line in company with the divisions of the flank.

Signals were most concerned with the wait for the favourable wind. An NCO from the Special Gas Co RE came down from GHQ and established himself at Div HQ. For over a fortnight he divided his time between recording observations of the wind and weather and exchanging messages with 'Meteor, GHQ' (the telegraphic address of the Meteorological Department) on the results of his labours. As all these messages had to be sent Priority and amounted sometimes to a score or more a day, the Signal Office staff were not wholly displeased to see the last of him, though personally he seemed a very nice fellow. After many postponements a seemingly favourable night for the attack was at length fixed upon. Just before the time came I was sent along to one of the brigades in case they should have need of an extra messenger and as I went there it was drizzling with rain. Hardly had I arrived when I heard that the gas had been discharged, had hung about No Man's Land and eventually rolled back on to trenches occupied by the division on the left, causing several casualties.

At the close of the year our sojourn at Sailly was almost at end. The only outstanding event during the remainder of our time there that I can remember is another bath. A bath in the vats of the Divisional Baths (like those at Sailly) was, however, not nearly such an inspiring business as those we got from time to time in real baths in civilian houses. The very routine, precise and rigid in every detail, coupled with the draughtiness of the place itself, which one encountered in Army baths, effectually damped the desires to whistle and shout and sing which a hot bath ought to instil into every normal person. The baths were approached by means of slippery duckboards in a surrounding sea of liquid mud.

Inside, the bather divested himself of his clothes, and walked naked along a cold concrete floor to a window where he handed in his undergarments in exchange for a cardboard ticket recording the number and nature of his discarded articles. This done, he walked back, shivering, to deposit his ticket in his tunic, and then set off for his bath. Arrived in the '*salle des bains*' proper, his next move was to decide which tub or vat he should patronise. More depended upon the soundness of his judgement in this matter than one would at first be led to imagine. Having bathed, he recommenced his nude wanderings, this time to another window where the tickets were exchanged for clean garments. During all this time the rickety sheds were being continuously shaken by the firing of our artillery ahead, but there was no reply from the German guns – at any rate not here.

Jan 12 (circa): The division moved out of the line and went into rear billets, becoming GHQ Reserve. The Div HQ went to Blaringhem taking over there from 8th Div who replaced us in the Sailly sector. The motorcyclists made the journey in groups at different times, and Smetham, Gripper and I made the journey together, via Estaires, Merris and Hazebrouck. Nearly all of us had accumulated such stocks of kit and belongings that when we moved our machines were drastically overloaded, though even then much had always to be left behind. I was one of the worst offenders in this respect and the weight at the back, combined with a slipping clutch and the now seldom-absent grease on the pavé resulted in the whole lot coming on top of me on more than one occasion during this ride. At Hazebrouck we made a short halt and I bought a pair of brown boots for 33 francs. The Army issue boots were very heavy, and being steel-shod made walking over pavé, especially if pushing a bike, a difficult and unpleasant matter.

On the Hazebrouck-St Omer road we came across part of a division just out from England. The troops were halted by the road (and all over it too) and extended a very long way.

At Blaringhem we took over the billet which had been occupied by the 8th Div DRs, but the place was so filthy and the old woman who ran it so confoundedly garrulous that the next day Smetham and Gripper and I sought shelter elsewhere and got a very excellent billet at the *Estaminet au Cheval Harnaché*. Unfortunately our move of lodging eventually got to the ears of the Camp Commandant, whose permission we had omitted to obtain and for this we were never forgiven by that gentleman who put us regularly ever afterwards into the worst places of all. 'Sufficient unto the day…' however and while we were at Blaringhem we three lived in luxury. I had the bed of honour, Smetham and Gripper reposed on mattresses on either side. The people of the estaminet were most hospitable and obliging and cooked our rations for us. It was here that I received the soubriquet, following Gripper's attempted translation of my name into French, of *le petit caporal.* It was bestowed on me by the youngest daughter of the house, who had a regular '*affaire de cœur*' with me, commenced by my presenting her with some chocolate. She was six years old and will be a handsome woman when she grows up.

While we were at Blaringhem we changed from the shift system of working to that of a roster of certain duties for each man each day. Under the new arrangement a DR would start the week with, say, all the regular runs to Corps throughout the day and nothing else, on the next day he might have two of the Brigade posts, the following day would be free until night duty, Thursday he would stand by for 'Specials', Friday he would have free to clean his machine and so on. We found it an improvement on the old plan.

The regular runs from here were:

3rd Corps	La Motte-au-Bois
Divisional Artillery HQ	Lynde
59th Brigade	Sercus
60th Brigade	Morbecque
61st Brigade	Steenbecque
Units at	Wittes

Jan 21: I got a night run to the HQ of 2nd Army, who lived in the big casino which is at the top of the hill on which lies the small town of Cassel. There is nothing so high or sudden as this hill for miles around and the panorama from the top is an extensive one, as I discovered on future visits in the daylight. The ascent to the town is very steep and full of hairpin bends. As I neared the top I was puzzled by a white light being waved to and fro ahead of me. It

proved to be a French sentry, waving his lantern to stop me, and from him I enquired the whereabouts of my destination. It was late when I got back and I didn't get much sleep, as we had orders to be ready to move from Blaringhem early the next morning. Life there was very tranquil and easy and we had looked forward to a month of it, but many rumours had been current the last few days, culminating in the order, at very short notice, to move. The whole idea of course of a 'GHQ Reserve' is to enable them to send troops rapidly to any place where they may be specially needed; moreover we were a 'Light' Division (the 14th was another), supposed to be able to move complete with more facility than an ordinary division.

Jan 22: The Division moved into the 2nd Army area – Div HQ established in the chateau at Oxelaere, at the foot of Cassel Hill. It was a cold frosty morning and several of us halted more than once on the way to drink from a thermos flask which I had recently received from home and had got the estaminet people to fill with hot coffee and rum.

The cooking and sleeping arrangements at Oxelaere were of the worst (the Camp Commandant being incensed over the Blaringhem incident); fortunately we found we could buy food and drink in fairly satisfying quantities at the sign of the *Pomme d'Or* in the village and got our meals here pretty regularly during the rest of our stay.

Jan 23: The state of our machines had grown from bad to worse. Many were unrideable (the lack of spare parts was still the principal source of trouble) and we had to take turns in riding what bikes were yet whole. My own had now been embellished with the legend 'Not to be ridden' and there was an immediate rush by the others for such parts as were serviceable. Mudguards, tyres, carburettor, oil-pump, gearbox and clutch, generator and finally clutch wire were each in turn exchanged for like articles which had become broken or damaged on the bikes of others. The result was a sorry sight. We heard that those whose machines were useless would be given horses, which made the majority of us anticipate more spills than ever. Meanwhile mounted sappers did a good deal of our work and we had a pretty easy time.

The chateau where we were was a typical, rather gimcrack looking edifice of this French type of residence; save for a caretaker it was empty. The grounds were quite jolly and must have been very fine in the summer: a clear stream ran through them, which considerably enhanced the effect and provided a ready solution to the problem of ablutions. The Signal Office personnel and Headquarters clerks, etc were in outbuildings in the grounds.

Two of us walked one evening to Bavinchove, where there were one or two very tiny shops, none of which sold anything of any use. From here, where is the railway station serving Cassel, a tramway runs up the hill to the '*Place*' of the town at the top. Once I saw a solitary tram, labelled '*Service de Gare et Ville*': it had broken down and the 'wattman' was underneath, leisurely tinkering. I don't think I ever saw one actually in motion.

Feb 1: Div HQ moved from Oxelaere to Esquelbecq. Smetham, as one of the senior DRs, was about to have a new bike, a consignment of which soon reached us. I was given his old one and sent off to the 61st Brigade at Arnèke. They were quartered in a large estaminet, which contained, so I was informed on my arrival, the prettiest girl and the largest stock of drinks that this section had ever met with. The place certainly boasted a good assortment of liquor for war-time, but I don't remember being particularly impressed with the lady.

Feb 2: The next morning the brigade moved off, en route for Wormhoudt and I was sent to the HQ of the Divl Mounted Troops (Westmorland & Cumberland Yeomanry) to be attached to them till they moved. They were at Rubrouck. Two of the Yeomanry DRs who were attached to us at Nouveau Monde, Rutherford and Hedley, were back with their unit, but their machines had been withdrawn and they were no longer acting as despatch-riders.

I got one or two runs to Division at Esquelbecq: for the only time for many months the roads were quite dry and riding was quite a pleasure, as the surface of most of the by-roads round here had been unspoilt by heavy traffic.

Feb 3: I was talking for some time with the corporal-clerk in the regimental 'office' and during our conversation he asked me, as everybody will, what part of England I hailed from. When I told him I'd lived many years in Derby, he asked if I were perchance the son of the Director of Education of the same name. O scion of an illustrious family! It appeared that in 'civvy life' he was in the Cumberland Education Office and had remembered the name from correspondence of an official nature. On the other hand the 'madame' of the estaminet where we were billeted, with whom I had long conversations on a great diversity of subjects, appeared to take it for granted that my father had so risen in the world as to have become a (presumably comfortable and well-to-do) proprietor of an estaminet. Was it my professorial mien, I wonder, that led her thus indirectly to compliment me? (I was often called 'The Professor', Heaven knows with what irony!)

Feb 5: The Yeomanry moved to Nachtigall Farm, near Esquelbecq. Hedley procured a Douglas from somewhere – he said it belonged to their colonel – and he and I accompanied them as motor cyclists during their move, after which I returned to Division at Esquelbecq. I found the DRs billeted in an estaminet on the corner of the market-place, kept by two of the most miserable old women it has ever been my lot to encounter. They groused and whined continuously, which made us very fed-up, for though the majority of us were young and we usually kicked up a good noise, most of the boys were very considerate fellows and honestly anxious to cause as little trouble as possible. We spent most of our leisure time feeding and playing billiards in other estaminets of the village. We were also good customers of a civilian barber's here, who though not a first-class hairdresser was superior in his methods to the signal company driver who ordinarily performed this office for us.

During the week we spent at Esquelbecq preparations were being made for our division to relieve the 14th Divn in the Canal Bank Sector of the Ypres Salient. The Skipper and a few men went up to that district and established a forward headquarters on the Poperinghe – Elverdinghe road. This was known as YTR (Y-Toc-R). YT was the Signals abbreviation for our division, Y being a Division, followed by T, the twentieth letter of the alphabet. Divisions having numbers beyond 26 had 3-letter code titles, thus the 29th Div for example would be YBI. The addition of the letter R signified Report Centre, hence YTR was 20th Divisional Report Centre or Forward Headquarters.

All commands from GHQ down to brigades were given distinctive signals code-letters in this manner. In the case of Armies and Corps the numerical letter preceded the letters AR and CO respectively (BAR = 2nd Army; CCO = 3rd Corps). In Brigades, whose distinguishing letters were Z for Infantry and F for Artillery brigades, the numerical letter came last, as with Divisions. The code calls of the three infantry brigades in our division were accordingly ZEI (59th), ZFZ (60th the second Z in this case standing for 0) and ZFA (61st).

Feb 9 (circa): I got a night run to the forward place, YTR. Smetham lent me his new machine, as the one I was using had got almost as bad as my original one. I went into Wormhoudt, Cassel and Poperinghe and as far as the latter place the roads were dry and very fair. From Poperinghe on however they were dreadfully greasy and progress was an absolute crawl. In Poperinghe I found one of our brigades who had come up and got some tea and further directions. The place, a few huts by the side of the road, was very hard to find. Eventually I got back about 2am.

Feb 11: The division moved. Div HQ established at YTR on Poperinghe – Elverdinghe road, about 3½ kilometres out of Poperinghe. One of the brigades had taken over on the left of the divisional sector the previous evening; the Boche had evidently got wind of the relief and had strafed them heavily, causing many casualties. This may have been due to spies, of whom there was a large number in this region, or to our haphazard use of the telephone in forward areas. We had not so far fully realised that a German listening set could pick up with ease spoken conversations at a distance of five or six hundred yards, and buzzer messages on earth return circuits (as were still frequently used) up to 1500 yards. Very little care was exercised over what was said on the telephone, even as far forward as battalions and companies; small wonder then that the Germans thus got to know of many movements of which we fondly imagined them to be completely ignorant.

The Fullerphone was introduced to overcome this difficulty, an instrument requiring a very small current for signals and in which the steady (Morse) current on the line (which is very difficult to 'pick up' on a listening set) becomes converted in the instrument to an interrupted current giving long and short buzzes. The early instruments of this type, however, were somewhat complicated and though they began to arrive about this time, they too often became relegated to the unused wagon down at the transport-lines. Later, however, they became universally used in forward areas and speech over lines within a certain distance from the front-line was stringently controlled.

REMEMBER EVERY WORD SPOKEN ON THIS TELEPHONE MAY BE OVERHEARD BY THE ENEMY. SAY NOTHING, THEREFORE, THAT YOU WOULD NOT SAY IN FRONT OF A GERMAN.

Conversation on private matters between individuals is strictly prohibited.

The following must never be mentioned, or even hinted at, over the telephone :—

1. Names (or numbers) of formations, units, commanders, billets, battery positions or O.P's.

2. Anything connected with reliefs, major or minor operations, raids, mining etc., either future or past.

3. Movements of troops or commanders.

4. Positions of dumps of stores and material, or the times at which rations, etc. are brought up.

5. Casualties sustained or ammunition expended.

Do not criticise the accuracy, or otherwise, of the enemy's fire.

Do not speculate about future events, even if you know nothing about them. By your conversation you may put the enemy on the right track and do your country an infinity of harm.

3rd Field Survey Co., R.E. 1847 18-7-17.

There seemed to be no place for our machines on our arrival at the new HQ (which was a collection of Army huts by the roadside). Later a shed was found further down the road. We had scarcely off-loaded our kit when Gripper and I were sent for to go round the Brigades to learn the route under the guidance of Spencer, who had preceded us some days before to get to know the district by living with 14th Div DRs (nearly all the latter, by the way, had

BSAs). Spencer assured us it was 'a proper joy-ride'. Our first halt was at one of our Field Companies, who were in the middle of a field of liquid mud at the corner of the road down to Elverdinghe. Then on to Elverdinghe where we turned to the right and were shown 'The Red House', headquarters of one of our artillery brigades.

The afternoon was sunny, but the pavé, which reached as far as Elverdinghe, was treacherous; our artillery kept up a most deafening din. They were in fact firing above the normal, in retaliation for the Boche's strafe of the previous evening; to us who had never encountered firing of this intensity and had just left the pastoral tranquillity of the rest area, it seemed a most unholy row. Boche shells we could see dropping on our left, but not close. Between Elverdinghe and Brielen we were stopped, owing to one of our batteries firing across the road. (This was in case of a possible premature.) We decided it was not a good place to stop, so we rode behind the battery, who were in a farm on the right of the road, over a ploughed field, through the farmyard and then across a ditch. Heaven knows how we managed it! There was no need for such haste, but the din and our inexperience had put the wind up us a bit, for which continuous motion was the best sedative. The canal-bank was reached by a road branching off 500 yards beyond Brielen, leading down to Essex Farm. This was always one of the most unhealthy bits of our route – indeed the road was universally known as Hell's Avenue.

We duly found the Left Brigade (59th) among the maze of dug-outs on the Canal Bank. The right Brigade was in process of relief, and 60th Bde HQ (who were taking over that sector) had not yet arrived. We were heartily glad to set off on the return journey, and scooted smartly up Hell's Avenue in spite of the whole distance of it being pitted with innumerable shell-holes of varying dimensions. On reaching the Brielen road at the top, Spencer was nowhere to be seen. The German shelling had increased considerably and several burst just then on the actual road behind us. We were just going to return, fearing he had got hit, when he hove in sight running with his machine. His belt had broken half-way up and he had, very naturally and wisely, deemed trundling his bike preferable to sitting down to a repair in that particularly objectionable spot. He arrived at the top purple in the face and almost done up with the exertion.

We got back late in the afternoon, not a little weary and terrifically hungry, as we had eaten nothing since leaving Esquelbecq and all the units we had called at, having only just arrived, appeared to be in the same predicament. There was nothing to be had at our cookhouse but we eventually got some tinned fruit at a fabulous price at a tiny shop down the road, about the most advanced spot reached by civilians in that neighbourhood. We were told to stand by and having filled up with petrol, we went to discover the hut allotted as our sleeping quarters. About 9pm I turned in, but was called out at 10 to take the evening Brigade post – Gripper being out on a run I was the only one available who knew the way. I had to wait an hour in the Signal Office before the post was ready and set off soon after 11.

The night was very dark and forward of Div HQ we were of course not allowed the use of headlights and riding on the pavé was very difficult and made more so by the stream of transport going in both directions which commences every evening at nightfall. The flash and crash of an HE [high explosive] shell by the road a short distance ahead at Elverdinghe served to remind me (if reminder were necessary) that these days were to be different days from those on the quiet Laventie front: it was followed shortly by others and I was nearly ditched by a scared mule. I got through Elverdinghe incredibly quickly and only remembered afterwards that the pavé there was so sticky that in the afternoon I had only dared to go through it at a slow crawl. At Brielen I passed a row of London motor-buses disgorging troops. Hell's Avenue was quiet and I delivered the Left Brigade stuff without further difficulty, but had a wearisome search for the Signal Office of the Right Brigade, who had not arrived when we were there in the afternoon. I was told the best way was to walk down the Canal Bank, so I left my machine with the 59th and started off down the duckboards, but they were packed with troops and progress was very slow. It was more than an hour later when I did at last find them and I then started to return to the other brigade for my bike, along the road.

Near Essex Farm the Boche started to send shrapnel over on to this road, which – as he knew very well – was at this time of the night full of transport. I retired to the lee of a tree trunk for shelter and ran into a Field Company corporal I knew, who had done the same. It didn't last very long, and having regained the Triumph, I was able, with the aid of a bit of moon which had sprung up, to get home at a fair speed. I got back, very tired, about 2am.

Feb 12: At 9 o'clock the next morning I was again deputed for the round of the brigades, this time to act as guide to Tulloch and Luise. By this time however I was getting inured to it, moreover I had had a meal and the artillery was much quieter. I quite enjoyed giving a somewhat exaggerated account of the perils of the route to my disciples before we started, even as our guide of the previous day had done to us. We did as a matter of fact get shelled on Hell's Avenue and had to time our walk from the machines into the various dug-outs and back in between salvoes, which were coming over pretty regularly about every 1½ minutes. I was riding Hippy's bike, which was fitted with T.T. bars and the darned thing refused to start each time that we were making our next little spurt forward. It fired eventually, fortunately on both occasions just in time for me to get away before the next lot. The speed at which we were often obliged to ride over these roads very soon broke all the spiral front fork springs of our Triumphs, one of the few weak points in their design. Most of us substituted a block of solid rubber cut from an old lorry tyre and kept it in place with a couple of stout straps.

Our new HQ gave us very little scope for off-duty hours, as Poperinghe was too far away and there was nothing of any interest on the spot. During the first few days, however, before the extra work entailed by the move had subsided, we were glad enough to spend it sleeping. We soon got used to the 'liveliness' of our runs, though several fellows had pretty close shaves at one time or another. One of the Brigade DRs got his machine smashed up with shrapnel, but fortunately was not on it at the time. Frequently however, our runs would be made without any sign of shelling en route. Div HQ was occasionally visited by German planes, who dropped a few bombs now and again but did not do any damage. The night runs to brigades were usually the worst, as then Hell's Avenue frequently came under the additional inconvenience of machine-gun fire. There was at this time a certain German machine gunner in the Salient who was notorious with the infantrymen in the line for his deadly aim and his own supernatural (so they said) immunity from being hit. He was known as Mad Alec and was reputed to be able to play tunes on his gun, so adept was he in its use.

Our regular runs during this period were as follows:

14th Corps	Lovie Chateau on the Poperinghe-Crombeke road
Guards Division	Town Hall, Poperinghe
84th Field Co RE	Outlying Fields
YTR	Trois Tours Chateau, near Brielen
Left Brigade	Canal Bank
Right Brigade	Canal Bank
Reserve Brigade	Rue d'Elverdinghe, Poperinghe

Routine stuff for Divisional units in and around Poperinghe were taken to the Reserve Brigade HQ, whence they were delivered by the Brigade motorcyclists and push-cycle orderlies. The principle ones not in Poperinghe itself were:

Divisional Supply Column	St Jan der Biezen
Ammunition Sub-Park	Watou
33 Mobile Veterinary Section	off the St Jan-Watou road.

Feb 14 (circa): Soon after our arrival in the Salient I was sent for a week to the Reserve Brigade in Poperinghe which at that time was 61st. The Signals section billet was in a not too whole house in the Rue d'Elverdinghe, where at one time or other a shell had landed in the back yard. Poperinghe had recently been paid considerable attention by a long-range gun on an armoured train in the vicinity of Roulers, but one of our batteries had apparently just succeeded in putting it, at any rate temporarily, out of action and for a while the town was immune from its unwelcome attentions. The Hun made up for this, however, by sending bombing planes over nearly every night when there was any moon. Whether the 'Taube' type of machine was used by the Germans for these expeditions I do not know, but at this period all German aeroplanes were 'Tawbs' to the British tommy. Smetham went on leave one night of this week and the Boche planes were, as usual, actively engaged in dropping their cargoes in the vicinity. His agitation and dread lest at the last moment the train should on this account get stopped were smiled at by some who had **not** got leave warrants for Blighty in their pockets; the station and railway lines generally were, of course, favourite targets for Fritz's 'eggs'.

I was told that one night when a warning had been received of the approach of a large number of hostile aircraft, the leave train was brought no nearer than Abeele, 6 kilometres back, for the sake of safety. By a tragic irony of fate the Boche also selected Abeele that night and bombed the train, inflicting many casualties, while Poperinghe station remained immune.

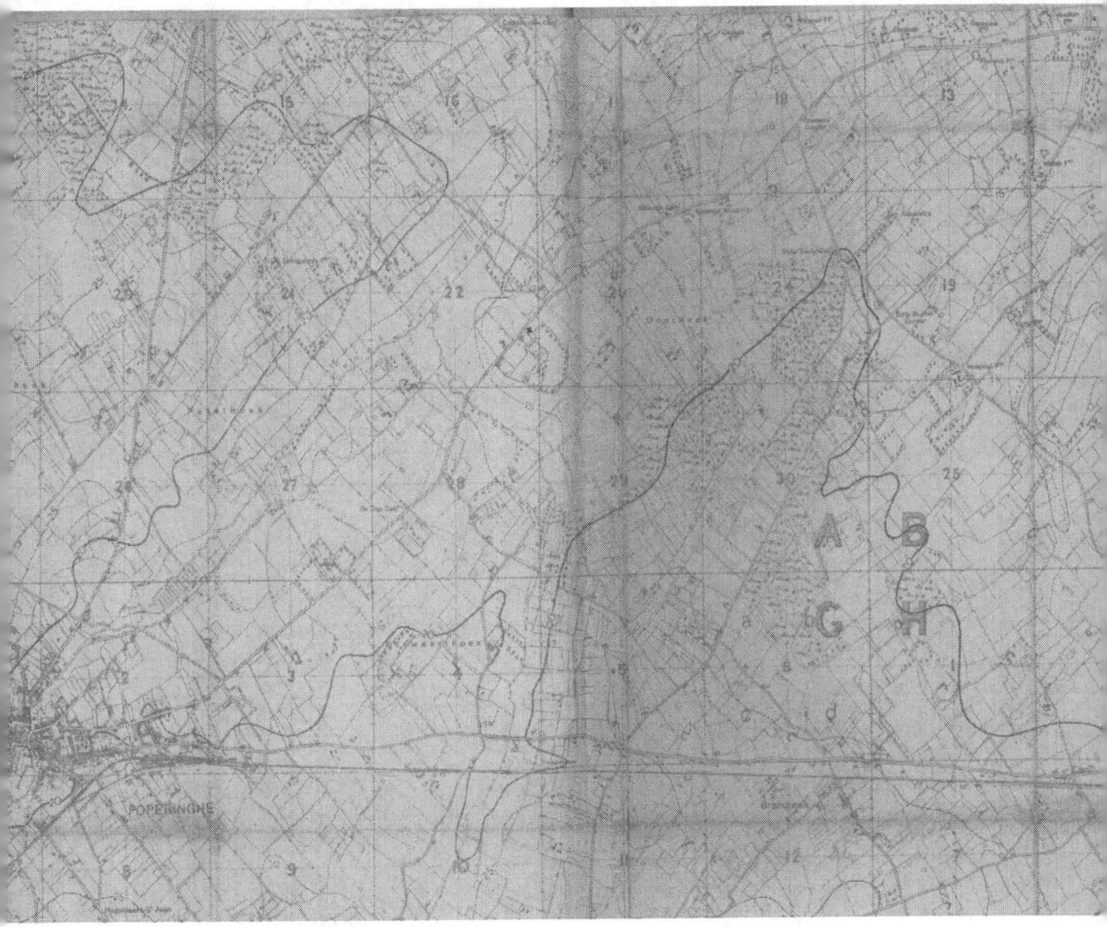

It is at Abeele that the Cassel-Poperinghe road crosses the Franco-Belgian frontier and though everyone was stopped and scrutinised here after dark, in the daytime military traffic passed unchecked and one could sail past the roadside *Douane* at a cheerful 25mph, a satisfaction (minute enough, indeed) which might have been put down to the credit side of war.

There was at this time in Poperinghe an excellent entertainment, known as the 'Fancies', run by officers and men of 6th Division, which we visited one night during my week in the town. As a means of providing an evening's interest, especially to the troops out of the line for a 'rest', its value was enormous and many of the songs and turns were quite equal to those on an English music-hall stage. The company included two Flemish girls, homeless refuges from Armentières, who went under the stage names of Phosgene and Lanoline. They could, however, neither sing nor act and were singularly destitute of good looks: their role was restricted to that of standing, with somewhat painful self-consciousness, at the back of the stage, where they formed a silent, and meagre 'chorus'.

The civilians of Poperinghe (at least those in the shops and estaminets, who were the ones with whom we came most in contact) were on the whole a singularly unattractive lot. There seemed to be many men still quite young, and their one idea appeared to be to fleece the British Army to the greatest extent possible. Flemish was the predominant tongue: most of the street and other public signs and notices were in this language. In a house on the opposite side of the road to our billet, from which we used to obtain water for washing and cooking, lived an old woman who kept a small oddment shop and with her I used to converse, with quite moderate ease, in a blend of German and Northcountry English. She told me some interesting tales of the town under German *régime*.

Feb 24: Back at Divl HQ employed as Signal Clerk in the Signal Office. The weather about this time became mighty wintry, with frost and snow – and what for us was even worse – the subsequent thaws. It lasted, intermittently at first, then pretty continuously, right on into March – almost till the end of that month in fact. The Signal Office, therefore was an acceptably dry and generally warm place to be in, and the following week I again escaped riding through being Orderly Corporal. Smetham arrived back hugely pleased with his leave and recounted meetings with the Hampstead folk and a lunch with EWS & LS [David's father & mother] at the University of London Club. Mac also came back from a special leave. Latterly he had been up with one of the brigades during a rough time and was recommended for a decoration. Just at this time however, all further leave was stopped.

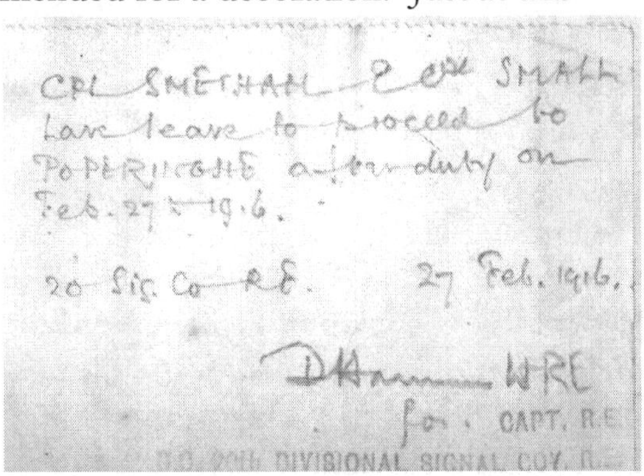
CPL SMETHAM & CPL SMALL
have leave to proceed to
POPERINGHE after duty on
Feb. 27th 1916.

20 Sig. Co R.E. 27 Feb. 1916.

for CAPT. R.E.
DIVISIONAL SIGNAL COY.

Mar 7: Again with Reserve Brigade in Poperinghe as motor-cyclist. The snow was thick and I had a beauteous night ride in it to the supply column who were now at

Herzeele. The approach to the Mobile Veterinary Sections, which had to be called at en route was rather a tricky one, down a narrow lane and ending up with two or three hundred yards to walk across fields from the road. Owing to the deceitful covering of snow, combined with the darkness and snowflakes driving in one's face, I was several times in the ditch down this road and eventually deemed discretion the better part of valour and made the rest of the way to the Mobile Veterinary on foot. Once back on the Watou road I got bad belt-slip, which grew steadily worse. The often successful dodge of tying a handkerchief round the countershaft pulley proved of no avail. The total distance of 8 miles to Herzeele was finally accomplished after 3½ hours of wearisome labour and I was so exhausted that I slept on the floor of the Supply Column orderly room just as I was until it was daylight again.

Mar 11: Finished reading EV Lucas' 'Listener's Lure', which I enjoyed immensely. The diversity of characters is remarkably well kept-up all through, though the 'letter-form' must be a difficult one to bring off successively. Some of the more 'philosophiky' portions reminded me a little of W J Locke, though the two writers as a whole are a complete contrast.

All this time Poperinghe came in for frequent attention from the Hun's long range guns (the Roulers one had apparently been replaced) and bombing planes. The gun-fire was usually concentrated pretty consistently on the eastern side of the town and the station, but occasionally I would be greeted with stray shots out on the Proven road when returning from my thrice daily run to the Supply Column. The 'Fancies' were still a source of attraction: 'Roger Run' was a great song and there was a new version of the old folk song 'I will give you the Keys of Heaven'. The lady (a pretty 'girl' with a squeaky voice) would listen to none of her lover's lures until at last:

'I will give to you a Whisky and Soda
I will give to you a Whisky and Soda
Madam will you walk, Madam will you talk
Madam will you walk and talk with me?'
whereupon 'she' promptly asserted her acceptance in a very deep basso!

The 'Fancies' were a great institution and one needed to have been out a good time to appreciate so thoroughly the type of sentimental song which at home one would probably have groaned to hear.

Mar 15: At long last I had become possessed of a new 1915 4hp countershaft Triumph, after many months of hacking about on a variety of decrepit and obsolescent specimens belonging to other people. It was a great acquisition, especially as for a few days we had quite decent weather and dry roads by way of a change. This day, knowing things to be slack for the moment at Brigade HQ, I made a run to one of the Field Ambulances (at Hilhoek, near Abeele) an excuse to try the paces of my new mount and journeyed on to Bailleul. Outside 2nd Corps HQ in the town I ran across Dark, for a long time one of our sapper telegraphists, who had been transferred to BCO Sigs. A little further on, outside the Canadian Corps HQ in the Town Hall I met one Cooke-Hill, OR, who was DRing with this crowd: he used to be in John Gould's house and was as far as I knew the only other Reptonian on the job besides myself. Allerley I saw there too – he was with us in England but did not manage to get out with us. He was their 'tiffy and came back part of the way with me to test one of the new 4-horse Douglases – it could go pretty fast, but I had no wish to exchange it for my Triumph.

Another day about this time I went off with Archie Gripper to allay hunger pangs at the YMCA canteen in Poperinghe. There was a most fearsome fug in the place, which was crowded with men all thanking their stars for its existence and we had quite a job to wangle our way through the crowd to the counter. There we demanded coffee from a good-natured looking individual garbed in a dirty white sweater, who with tousled hair was perspiringly operating a row of steaming urns. Something about him seemed familiar and we found ourselves staring at each other – almost immediately then I recognised him as Elmsley of Christ's, who had benevolently asked me to brekker one morning of my first term at Cambridge. The *rencontre* resulted in Archie and I having supper with the workers of the canteen after their day's toil was over, which was a pleasant change.

Mar 20 (circa): Returned to Division and went on duty in the Signal Office. By this time we had got a wireless installation at Divl HQ, nominally as part of a scheme of auxiliary communication within this and the neighbouring divisions, but more interesting to us as a receiver of the various official communiqués, including the German ones. I was given the job of translating the latter for the benefit of the staff, who liked to have them read at breakfast. During this month Gen Davies, the Divisional Commander was succeeded by Gen Douglas-Smith. Colonel Kenyon, the CRE also left the division about this time.

Mar 29: Having been instructed to return to motorcycling duties, I cleaned my machine and did one run to rear units, quite a pleasant one with sun and dry roads, only to find on my return that my successor in the Signal Office (who was also a DR) had committed some faux pas and been 'struck off the roster for duty in the Signal Office'. So I was re-installed, just in time to go on for the all-night shift – which had the merit however of providing time for thought (if one had inclination, which was not always) and for working off arrears of correspondence. This night Smetham had the 9pm Brigade 'Post' (never an enviable run in this part of the world) and at the far end, when he returned from the Brigade Signal Office to the spot on the road where he had left his bike, found the latter had been run down and smashed up by a motor ambulance. A disheartening discovery at any time, but in that particular quarter it was never advisable to remain on that road for longer than was absolutely necessary. The previous night, too, had seen the Brigade Post DR run into by a car, to the detriment both of himself and his machine, the latter's damage was, fortunately, the worse of the two.

A greater casualty than these had occurred a few days before, when Captain Huddlestone of the 84 Field Company was killed. He had been one of my 'pupils' at Larkhill and was a fine gentleman and a gallant officer. Our Field Companies had seen an almost total change of officers since the arrival of the division in France, but the Signal Company had thus far been lucky in the matter of casualties, three other ranks having been wounded. A few days before this Dick Goode, then a sapper with the 61st Bde, was awarded the DCM for repairing lines under heavy fire.

Mar 31: I had of late been feeling a considerable amount of strain in the eyes, with blurred visions and the like from time to time, so I obtained leave to be examined by an oculist to see if I could get a remedy. For this purpose I journeyed from Poperinghe to Hazebrouck by train – the first time I'd been in one since our journey up-country the previous July. The line in question, really belonging to the Nord-Belge, was one of those which has been taken over and were being worked by the Railway Operating Division, RE. They had imported a number of English locomotives from various railways and I saw some very large tank engines of a type unfamiliar to me. Like all the others taken over by these people they had been painted black and displayed 'ROD' in huge white letters. Sauntering along in this train at a placid 12 miles an hour (it was composed of antiquated French passenger rolling stock, a remarkable luxury for other ranks in those days) brought back many memories of continental journeys in more happy-go-lucky and seemingly far-off times.

Hazebrouck station was the scene of much traffic; trains full of French and English units on the move and a host of station officials, English, French and Belgian soldiers and police, with an odd 'civvy' or two here and there. I saw one of the fine new English-built Ambulance trains, consisting entirely of bogie corridor coaches – a great contrast to the prevailing type of continental railway carriage. It was brought in by an 0-6-0 Belge loco displaying the words '*Admis à ciculer sur le reseau du Nord*', and was taken on by a 4-cylinder compound Nord engine, 4-6-0, of enormous size. Both locomotives and of course each coach, displayed a large red cross. The train had probably come down from the St Remy CCS near Poperinghe. Having found and reported at the clearing hospital in Hazebrouck and been sent to the Ophthalmic Ward thereof, I found the doctor in charge a Cambridge man and pleasant to talk to; his verdict was that nothing was seriously wrong, but that I needed a tonic! I told him leave would be the best tonic, to which he agreed, but all he did for me was to write a brief note to the MO of the 20th Div REs which I ultimately exchanged for some very ordinary looking pills. These were the requisite 'tonic'. He did indeed offer to keep me under treatment for a few days, but I didn't relish the atmosphere of the place and returned 'home' the next day.

Apr 1: As we leisurely crawled through the intermediate stations on the return journey – Caëstre for instance and Godewaersvelde, ordinarily the scene of a customs examination – I was struck with envy of their military personnel – an RTOs job at Caëstre, thought I, was Paradise indeed. And yet I doubt not that many a member of the PBI [poor bloody infantry], seeing us slide off back to the rear on excellent bikes, has been likewise struck with the 'cushiness' of **our** lot.

Apr 3: I was admitted into the 61st Field Ambulance, which was just opposite Div HQ, with a touch of 'flu (so much for the 'tonic' pills!). The 'beds' consisted of stretchers supported on trestles and I was promptly ordered a 'No 9' by the MO on duty, Lt. Maling who had been awarded the VC for heroic work during the Battle of Loos. Things were not so bad here, however, as I had many visitors from the Company who used to pop across every now and then to see how I fared and, thanks to the excellent Army postal service and those wonderfully thoughtful people of Hampstead, I was the daily recipient of ever welcome letters, papers and parcels.

Apr 6: Div HQ shelled during the morning. The first shells landed a few yards beyond the hutments which constituted the Ambulance 'wards'. Tender enquiries as to whether the Hun would lengthen or shorten his range! Fortunately for us, he did the former and the next one pitched just by the Signals Mess at Div HQ, smashing much crockery but causing no casualties.

Apr 11: My temperature being somewhat reduced, I was permitted to get up and – so as to leave another bed vacant for urgent cases coming down the line – was packed off to the Divisional Rest Station. This inappropriately named unit was situate at Hilhoek and cannot have been more than five or six miles back from the Field Ambulance, yet the journey thither took nearly two hours in a crawling and cumbersome old horse ambulance, whose only merit was that it was rubber-tyred. Arrived there we shiveringly awaited (there were several other convalescents with me) the arrival of the MO on duty, in the draughty Reception Hut. After a good deal of messing about, we were allotted to our various sleeping huts and told to have a bath. This operation consisted in waiting in a hut ten times draughtier than the reception hut until one of the wooden tubs in the next compartment was vacant and then attempting to get clean in a tepid mixture of dirty water and disinfectant. Meals in the DRS were obtained after a long wait in a queue in a particularly biting east wind. A day and a half of this salubrious resort convinced me that Hilhoek was no place for anyone trying to throw off influenza so on the morning of 13th I assured the MO when he came on his daily rounds, in as breezy and assured a tone as I could muster, that I was perfectly fit and desired nothing so ardently as to be 'returned to unit', a statement that was at least partly true. So back I went and though feeling extremely dicky, I was very glad to get amongst the boys again. Hippy considerately put me on duty in the Signal Office. Leave, which had started again recently, I found had been once more stopped. I endeavoured to make up for my recent starvation diet and to put new life into myself by guzzling the contents of many welcome parcels of groceries from home.

Apr 16: The Skipper got his majority, which we are all pleased about. His energy was positively amazing and after working hard all the day and evening he would always come into the Signal Office between 1 and 2 am each night and read through all the day's messages. The Division was now in process of being relieved by 6th Div and went back for a month's rest and on the next day Div HQ moved back to Esquelbecq.

Apr 17: Most of the DRs who were not actually on duty went there in a body and we stopped at Cassel on the way and had an excellent feed in a hotel in the square. To partake of a meal of many courses at a table decked with tablecloth and napkins, cutlery and clean plates was a huge luxury. At Esquelbecq we avoided that misnomer, the *Café de l'Harmonie*, where we had been billeted on the previous occasion and got a billet in another estaminet on the other side of the road – at least Hippy, Smetham, Archie and I went there and the rest were scattered about near at hand. Archie had procured a Decca gramophone which made us very cheery - besides a goodly selection of rag-time there were some first rate records of such items as Järnefelt's Praeludium, Boccherini's Minuet, Liszt Rhapsodies and so forth, which it was a huge pleasure to hear again.

Apr 23 Easter Day: The assemblage of villagers outside the church and the sounds of the organ coming forth seemed almost theatrical and might have been a scene from Cavalleria Rusticana. One or two of us tried to get to one of the services, but their times clashed with our duty hours. Later on during this stay at Esquelbecq however, I did go to mass one morning (May 14th). After the morning service the people dispersed and within the houses there was much ceremonial eating of heavy cake and drinking red wine. In our billet those of us who were there at the time were invited to be present and the repast took place in a somewhat strained silence, the visitors in their best clothes sitting very straight and prim all round the room.

Apr 24: As a result of an enquiry for NCOs and men 'with a good knowledge of colloquial German' I suddenly found myself ordered to report at 14th Corps HQ (Intelligence) for examination. The OC must have sent in my name, though Heaven knows I knew next to nothing of colloquial German and such German as I did know I had mostly forgotten. However I was not sorry as I had no wish to leave the company and no particular desire for the job I imagined these men to be required for – duty with a forward listening-set. The territorial lieutenant who interviewed me at Corps seemed rather to hanker after me, however, in spite of the fact that I could hardly muster enough spoken German for a consecutive sentence, so I endeavoured to deter him with a fictitious story of applying for a commission (at least it was brought out on the spur of the moment, but it gave me an idea which I subsequently followed up). When I got away I went back via Poperinghe and Cassel, stopping at the latter town for another feed and also a bath. The spring sun and the fresh green of the trees and fields, and the song of many birds, made the ride quite a good one.

Apr 25: For several weeks, partly owing to my dose of flu, I had been on duty in the Signal Office. I was now due to got out as a motorcyclist to one of the brigades, but Mac developed diphtheria (and, incidentally, got back to Blighty) with the result that the rest of us in our billet were put in semi-isolation and my visit to the brigade was postponed.

Apr 26: Inoculated (paratyphoid). The French papers at this time were full of reports of the Russians landing in France, giving even their supposed places of destination.

May 1: During this period of rest the Division was first of all in GHQ, then in Corps Reserve and each brigade went in turn to Calais for a period of a week or ten days each. Each day there was one run to this brigade at Calais from Div HQ, which was taken by each of the DRs in turn. My turn at length arrived – it was a trip we all looked forward to, as we left Esquelbecq at 10am and did not start back from Calais until 4pm, thus getting some free time there for shopping and eating (the latter usually had priority). My ride thither was accomplished in very good weather and the roads were dry. I went via Bourbourg and Gravelines and noticed a large number of Belgian troops in this district, apparently having a pretty good time. Brigade HQ were established at the Grand Hotel, a very luxurious establishment. It was reported that after a few days the Brigade staff were compelled to move to cheaper quarters. I had an excellent lunch at a restaurant in the '*Place d'Armes*', but an extensive ride round the town which I had promised myself during the interval of waiting was checked by a heavy thunderstorm. I felt aggrieved at this, as all the DRs who had made this trip on the preceding days had had beautiful weather all the time. However, I lingered over lunch (and it was not a bit dull, for the sight of civilian men and women dressed in any degree of smartness and elegance was a very novel one. It was curious to reflect that 50 miles away were the front line trenches). Then I made a round of the shops and acquired a few new records for our gramophone, besides a variety of stationery and picture postcards and the like. By the time I set off on the return journey the rain had stopped and though the roads were wet the day ended with a very beautiful evening and a gorgeous sky.

May 9: My put-off turn with a brigade had materialised and I was at Houtkerque with first of all 59th and then 61st Bde. Here I managed to get a good billet in a cottage with a bedroom to myself, which I took over from the DR I relieved. It was a typical French wooden bedstead, with large and lofty mattresses and very small bedclothes, but after the first night when my predecessor (I cannot remember now who it was), who did not return to Div until the following morning, shared the bed with me (but not the bedclothes), it was luxurious to a degree. It rained most of the time here, which made the evening run into Esquelbecq unpleasant and a series of punctures capped my disgust. On 13th I was relieved and returned to Div. Two days later occurred the first fatality among the DRs. It was ironical that it should occur when we were far from shot and shell. A young fellow named Bowring had been sent up from the base a few days previously to replace Crummack and for the first few days worked at HQ with Adam Tindall the 'tiffy to get a little acclimatised to new surroundings. For this reason several of us, myself included, had hardly met him, but by all accounts he was an extremely decent, quiet sort of boy.

May 15: And this night, when he had only just commenced to do regular riding duty, he collided with a sidecar belonging to the Supply Column on the Wormhoudt road. It was dark of course and what really happened most of us never knew, but apparently he was thrown on to the line of the light railway *(Chemins de Fer Economiques du Nord)* running at the side of the road and was run over and instantly killed by a passing train. He was buried the next day in the village cemetery at Esquelbecq. It was a very simple and touching ceremony, the body on a stretcher, covered with a blanket and a Union Jack, borne by four of us to the graveside and many of the villagers who attended were deeply affected.

Before we left Esquelbecq each DR was put on to do duty in the stables, under the theory (a very just one) that as we were corporals and frequently did regimental duties as such, we ought to have some idea of the other jobs prevailing in that most many-sided of units, a Signal Company. There was not a little grousing, nevertheless, at having to turn out at an early hour in the morning, walk half a mile to the wagon lines, and start 'mucking-out' unwilling horses or even more unwilling mules. Still, if the drivers did it every morning there was no reason why we shouldn't be able to do it. But (we would argue perversely) the drivers live on the spot, they can at any rate have 10 minutes more between the blankets! A good many of us had never been on a horse in our lives and if the uninitiated way in which we performed our stable duties at first earned the disgusted maledictions of those in charge, our trials and woes when it came to exercising them afterwards at any rate provided them with some amusement by way of recompense.

The first time I got let in for this, the file of mounted men were already leading out on to the road before ever I had succeeded in girthing up and getting my harassed animal on to the parade ground. Some friendly drivers gave me a leg up (the brute was so much higher than a Triumph and not nearly as steady) and followed by stentorian shouts of 'Good old Tiny' 'Don't let 'im run away wiv you, Tiny' and 'come and look at old Tiny on a bleedin' 'oss' I followed desperately in the wake of the others. Or rather the aptly described animal I was on followed them. I had nothing to do with it. Trial No 1 was immediately outside, in the form of a company or more of French infantrymen who were halted on each side of the road. But I stuck on and anyway it amused them. Trial No 2 was a shrieking light railway locomotive that hove in sight without any warning whatever. There were countless other trials, but I did eventually reach the rest. Nevertheless I was exceedingly thankful to see the wagon-lines loom into view again on the return journey.

May 20: The division was again preparing to return to the line and Hippisley and I were ordered to proceed to Poperinghe on the next day and take over the Signal Office from the Onards Division, preparatory to our division taking over the Ypres sector from them.

May 21: This we duly did, but having been given no definite time to report, we made an expedition to Dunkerque on the way in order to have a final good meal there. The streets of the town were covered with broken glass as the result of an air raid the previous night, which we had seen – the glare of fires and bursting archie shells – from our billet at Esquelbecq. We had no authority to be there, but never dreamt of meeting with anyone who would know us and after an aperitif in a café, we swaggered into the *salle à manger* of the principal hotel and ordered lunch. We had barely started it when who should come to almost the very next table but several of the red-tabbed members of our own divisional staff. They stared a little at seeing a corporal and sergeant (and they must have recognised us) so near, but we brazened it out and had an excellent meal. We never heard anything further of the incident and duly took over our Signal Office in Poperinghe.

May 22: The division came in the next day – Div HQ and Signals were in Poperinghe Town Hall and at first the NCOs, DRs and sappers of the Signal Co were billeted at the top of the building, but afterwards moved to the shell-shocked house in the Rue d'Elverdinghe which used to be our Reserve Brigade HQ.

The regular runs were:

Brigades in the Ramparts at Ypres, calling at YTR at Vlamertinghe and at the Town Major of Ypres in Ypres Prison
14th Corps – Lovie Chateau
Div Supply Column – Herzeele

At this time the Boche artillery used generally to be pretty busy and the back areas got raked at any rate as far as Poperinghe. We had one or two disquieting nights at our billet, where we slept upstairs – the fellows in the Town Hall however had some fine vaults to go to on these occasions in the basement of the building, a refuge also used by civilians in the town. The latter apparently used to take refreshment along with them there and we used to hear great stories of champagne orgies and so forth, which led some of the Rue d'Elverdinghe folk to vow they would change their billet!

May 28: Two new DRs arrived up from the base one day at the end of May during a shelling of the town and seemed to think it a horrible reception and were no better pleased the next day when I led them round the brigades – Fritz being again busy. This shelling reached its culminating point a few days later (June 2), when there was a strafe between the Canadians and the Boche at Hooge, the latter getting into the 'village'. (It was no more than a name – and some trenches, and I think its determined retention by us up to then was largely sentimental, for it made a bulge out of our line.)

The road from Vlamertinghe to Ypres (which formed the 'bottle-neck' of the Salient and was our only route to the town) was badly shelled and I had an exciting trip with the 2 o'clock Brigade Post. Shortly after leaving Vlamertinghe at the beginning of the part of the road then being shelled, I found a Canadian DR halted by the side of the road and found he had broken his front fork-spring. It seemed a strange place to stop for that mishap – he told me he'd sent a message by another DR asking for a new one to be sent to him. I offered him a strap to put round his forks as a temporary measure, but no, he would have it that he was going to wait there for his new spring. It was no place to stop arguing with an obstinate loon, who I suppose knew his own business best, so yelling to him above the din that whoever brought his spring (if they ever did) would be lucky if they didn't have to carry away his corpse, I made on. The road was strewn with leafy tree-branches which had been shot down and I could see them coming down ahead of me, but I got to the ramparts all right and called at the Left Brigade first and then on to the Right Brigade. Here I found all wires to the Brigade Signal office had been cut by shellfire – the brigadier and the brigade major had both been wounded on a tour of inspection and had just returned to HQ. There I had to wait while they wrote out accounts of the progress of events and suggestions for reinforcements for the Canadians for me to take back to division.

While there in the Signal dug-out there was a colossal crash above and one of the towers of the Eglise S. Jacques close by came crashing down, the debris just missing my bike which I'd left outside. Before I left, the Signal Officer came in and bade me a solemn goodbye and good luck and implored me not to get knocked out before I'd handed over my stuff at Poperinghe Town Hall. When I eventually got away, I had a return ride as exciting as the way out – this time I didn't attempt to dodge along by timing the salvoes, but blinded along all-out. I remember being amused by the grim and set expressions of such DRs as I passed on the road – probably mine was not unlike them. When I at last got back, the durability of the Triumph and especially of its valves when ridden at high speed, had risen high in my estimation.

This fighting slackened the next day and June 4th and 5th were comparatively quiet on 20th Div front.

I had thought from time to time more or less seriously of applying for a commission, partly because I had got very interested in the work of the many different sides of a Divisional Signal Company, partly too in a vague hope of getting sent to England for training and thus wangling a leave and one day I had gone before the CO and suggested the possibility to him. He offered to attach me to one of the Brigade Sections to get some practical experience in line work (Crummack had been doing this for a similar end before he got diphtheria) and on June 3 I went up to Left Brigade HQ in the Ramparts. The shelling had not yet ceased and a good many barrages were put down, some of tear gas. The 59th Bde were the Left Brigade at this time and on the following day I was out on lines with Sgt Peart – best of good fellows, who was killed not long after I'd left the division. The shelling had quieted down and the weather was glorious, but rations were scarce, owing to the difficulty of getting them up the last few days and food parcels from home were consequently much appreciated.

The HQ of the Bde had previously been on the canal bank and when they moved to the ramparts, the existing brigade lines were taken there in 3 'quads', suspended along the canal side – in many places they were right at the bottom of the canal. On June 8-9 we hauled these out of the water and for some distance buried them under the setts at the edge of the quay. The same day (June 8) the line from Bde HQ to Left Group Artillery went dis, and in the evening we laid an emergency line of D1 cable. This was replaced two days later by a permanent spare earth-return line of D5 cable. This was a straightforward ground cable laid across country, but necessitating a good many buried crossings.

This sort of routine work and patrolling of lines, I did for about three weeks, thus on June 11 we reeled up the emergency line laid on the 8th, which had already got cut by shell fire in several places and went out on a ditch line to the Reserve Battalion at the Prison, which had a troublesome fault. This was also a D5 earth-return line. On 12th we were out at the Test Point at St Jean (where a couple of linemen used to be stationed) reconnoitring a route for a new line from Bde which should avoid the quads in the canal. Two days later (June 14) we were out labelling lines and salving cable from unlabelled and unused ones. On 23rd we were on the same sort of job, this time in a communication trench – 'Haymarket' leading to Battn HQ at Potijze - running from the front line to Battalion HQ – clearing lines and making them run together the length of the trench. (A recent Corps Order had been issued to the effect that all wires remaining unlabelled after a certain date were to be picked up by the Div Signal Co.)

When at Bde HQ I became a disciple of Nash – PO man and Office Sergeant at Bde Signals, and Miles, the instrument Corporal, who both taught me a good bit about instruments and testing.

An emergency visual scheme had been prepared from the Bttns to Bde, which was tested every evening. A Brigade visual station was manned on the ramparts above Bde HQ and would receive at 9 each evening a message from Right Bttn HQ and at 9.15 one from Left Bttn. As signals from Bde Lamp Stn were pretty certainly visible by the Boche, DD working was used, each group signalled twice and was written down as sent. When received Bde Stn sent general answer (instead of the old 'RD') which was the only signal it sent.

At this time Ypres itself was usually pretty quiet except for a morning and evening 'hate' – on June 23 Heilgers, who was DR attached to the brigade at the time and I made a tour of the town and explored the ruins of the Cathedral and the Cloth Hall. One evening a little later we explored the shattered railway station and annexed as souvenirs some tickets from the ruins of the booking office and a large enamelled iron placard which prohibited, in Flemish, an unhygienic practice and which we added to the furniture of our dugout.

June 24: A new dugout has been made in the front line as battle headquarters for a strafe which was arranged for the next night and a special line was required to it from brigade. Peart and I were on this job and started the line from the forward end, laying what was known as a 'substitute', a twisted pair of single strand copper which broke very easily. From Bttn HQ to Bde we utilised existing lines. The cable we had with us was insufficient and we finished it the following morning (June 25) with D5. The staff apparently wanted the line so as to get direct news of the progress of the raid (it was made by the 10 KRRs and was supposed to be pretty successful), but as a matter of fact it went dis before they started. Two linemen were on the job of maintaining the forward part – Coleman and 'Sooner Hollands' – with their headquarters at the Test Point. The Boche artillery soon retaliated and the line got cut to bits – poor Bob Coleman was killed and Hollands wounded trying to get it through again: Hollands got the MM for his work on this occasion.

June 26: When Peart and I went out the next morning to start reeling the line up again, we found the communication trench up which it was laid in some places scarcely recognisable and for nearly its whole erratic course the Hun gunners had 'taped' it with amazing accuracy. We felt it was a heavy price to pay for a line on which, so far as we knew, no real issue depended and which in fact had gone dis before it was really required at all.

June 30 (circa): About two days later 59th went out of the line into rest billets on the Crombeke road at Poperinghe and I returned to Div HQ and DR duty. My headlamp wanted a new glass door (July 2) and as we had no spares, I got a pass one day in the succeeding week to go to the Divisional Supply Column at Herzeele for a new one. When I got there they had no glass doors but provided me with a new lamp (which incidentally was of a much better type than the old). It was a lovely day and I was not on duty till 10pm so, as

I'd passed moving troops on the way to Herzeele, I thought I'd go back by a different (and less direct) way, so having fixed on the lamp I went on through Wormhoudt to Cassel, where I went to our favourite hotel in the *'place'* and had a five course lunch. The day was called by the French 'Procession Sunday' and every place had the French flag floating from the windows and was full of girls and children dressed and veiled in white. In one village the road was strewn with all kinds of greenery, including rose branches which I didn't much appreciate.

July 4: While taking the Brigade post to Ypres I got caught (without overcoat) in a tremendous thunderstorm and was completely drenched. The Boche was sending over HE but the sound was drowned by the thunder, which gave you an unpleasantly helpless sensation.

July 5: The next day I went up to Bde again for more line work, this time to the Right Brigade. The 60th were in at the time but were relieved a little later by the 61st. Brace, the Signal Officer of the 60th took me with him early the next morning on a tour of inspection – to the Bttn HQ in Railway Dugouts (beyond Hell Fire Corner) etc.

July 7: At 10.30pm I had to go with the bike to Potijze as orderly to the Staff Captain of the Left Brigade, while gas cylinders were brought up in lorries, offloaded and taken on down a communication trench to the front line by infantry carrying parties, in readiness for a raid to be done by the 59th. The unloading was supervised by NCOs from the RE Special Gas Cos. There was a desultory whizzbang shelling going on and there was a certain amount of wind-up lest one should drop on a cylinder and free the contents. As far as I could gather my duty if this occurred was to go forward to the front line and back to Bde HQ simultaneously, shouting 'Gas'! I wonder how far I should have got.

July 8: My 21st birthday. Several presents had come from England during the last few days, some edible, others an oilskin, a book and a fountain pen. I got leave to go to Poperinghe on the excuse of a bath and met Welsford, who stood me a birthday dinner (at Skindles, where we used to go in a back room and feed as the officers did but *à meilleur marché*. 'Champagne' was 4fr a bottle). I afterwards met divers other divisional DRs and eventually, greatly cheered, returned to Ypres, to find a heavy bombardment going on.

This, when I'd managed to get back to the Ramparts, gave me pleasant thoughts for the evening when last night's gas stunt was to be repeated. However, the shelling got a good deal quieter about 9pm. But as I was standing by, at Potijze, in a ruined cottage where I had put my bike, a series of whizzbangs came over of which one at least (two I believe) hit the building and brought down a shower of splinters and debris. I was pretty scared but seemed to be otherwise all right – shortly after however I started to have trouble with a finger of the right hand – whether coincidence or whether some abrasion made by falling debris got poisoned I don't know. Anyway my hand and arm soon swelled up and were mighty painful and when I got back to Bde Jimmie Ritchie filled a gumboot with boiling hot water and made me keep them soaking in it, for which I've always been grateful to him.

July 9: At 4am I went off to the Field Dressing Station in the Prison on the other side of the town, where they put a fomentation on for me and 24 hours later (July 10) having had no sleep, went again. This time I was held up for several hours owing to the town being shelled and a barrage being put on the roads. When I got to the Dressing Station I found one of the divisional linemen, Poynter - lying on a stretcher, having been hit while out on one of the lines near Ypres – he was pathetically cheerful, but died soon afterwards. During these two days I rode when necessary but with the arm in a sling, but I wasn't good for much work and on 12th went down to a Field Ambulance at Poperinghe. I spent the night in the DRs billet and arrived just in time for a long range strafing of the town – 43 shells, of which 38 were duds.

July 13: I was admitted into a Field Ambulance on the Watou road and Welsford proved himself the kindest hearted of fellows, rough diamond though he was. He carted my kit for me, shaved me and generally made things as easy as possible. The town was again shelled and all troops were ordered out of the town.

July 16: I was transferred by motor ambulance to Wormhoudt, feeling very fed up with the whole business and being amongst strangers. The next day I was moved again, this time to the Casualty Clearing Station at S. Remy, near Poperinghe. From here I went down by hospital train as a stretcher case to Calais, where I was sent to 35th General Hospital and finally from there to England, arriving in Keighley Hospital 5am on July 21st.

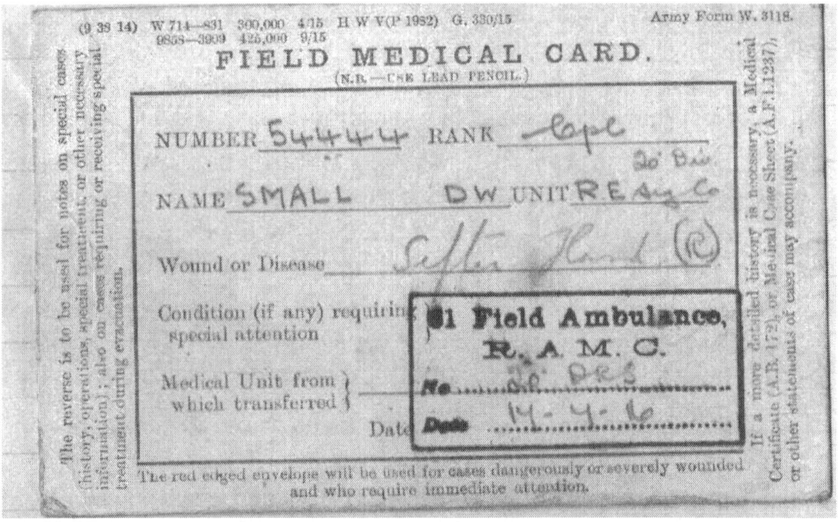
(9 38 14) W 714—831 300,000 4/15 H W V(P 1982) G. 330/15
9858—3909 425,000 9/15
Army Form W. 3118.

FIELD MEDICAL CARD.
(N.B.—USE LEAD PENCIL.)

The reverse is to be used for notes on special cases (history, operations, special treatment, or other necessary information); also on cases requiring or receiving special treatment during evacuation.

NUMBER 54444 RANK Cpl
NAME SMALL DW UNIT RE Arty Co 20 Div
Wound or Disease Septic Hand (R)
Condition (if any) requiring special attention
Medical Unit from which transferred
Date

61 Field Ambulance, R. A. M. C.
No 20 DRS
Date 14-4-16

If a more detailed history is necessary, a Medical Certificate (A.B. 172), or Medical Case Sheet (A.F.I.1237), or other statements of cases may accompany.

The red edged envelope will be used for cases dangerously or severely wounded and who require immediate attention.

C Ward, Morton Banks Hospital

David Small in back row between Nurse Powell-Harries and Nurse Scatterty (daughter of Senior MO)

Theatre Staff, Morton Banks Hospital: Dr Dobey & Nurse Prince-Smith (standing centre and right)

C Ward, Keighley Hospital 1916

Wounded soldiers from the Bradford and Keighley hospitals were the guests of the Bradford Athletes' B
West Riding Volunteers at a military gymkhana held in Myrtle Park, Bingley, on Saturday. The upper pho
the officers, Sub-Commandant Hazley (who was in command) being in the middle of the front row. A batch of
are shown in the lower picture.

rkshire Observer" copyright.

1917

Jan: At Houghton Regis Signal Depot, Dunstable, a member of the Permanent Motorcycle Guard. Came here after 3 months at Keighley and sick leave. Marked for Home Service by Medical Board.

Feb 17: Joined S27 Cadet Class at Haynes Park (Cable and Riding).

Mar 19: Dunstable portion of course began (Air line, electrical theory).

Apr 9: Visual and Trench (Bde Section) portion of course began.

Jul 29: Wireless course at Malvern.

Aug 1: Commissioned (Gazetted Aug 23).

Sep 1: To Bedford.

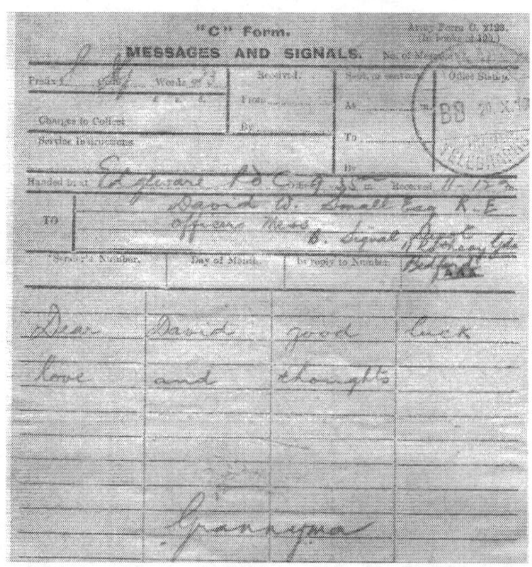
"C" Form.
MESSAGES AND SIGNALS.

Prefix | Words | Received | Office Stamp
Charges to Collect
Service Instructions
Handed in at: Edgware P.O.
TO: David W. Small Esq R.E.
Officers Mess, B. Signal Depot
Bedford
Sender's Number | Day of Month | In reply to Number

Dear David good luck
love and thoughts

Grannyma

Oct 12: Warned for draft.

COPY.

121/Draft etc/7130 (A.G.7).

WAR OFFICE,
LONDON, S.W.1.
22nd Oct.1917.

Sir,

Lieuts.
D.A.Porteous.
A.E.Villiers.

2/Lts.
D.W.Small.
E.W.Plowman.

x On 26th Oct. Train leave Victoria at 7.35a.m.

With reference to the orders for the officers of Royal Engineers named in the margin to hold themselves in readiness to proceed overseas, I am directed to request that you will issue instructions to these Officers to proceed to Folkestone (x). They should be provided with the necessary railway warrants, the number and date of this letter being quoted on the warrants as authority.

On arrival at Folkestone the officers should report themselves personally to the Assistant Embarkation Commandant for passage. Embarkation has been authorised.

The date of the departure of the officers should be reported by letter to A.G.7., War Office.

The above information is to be at once communicated through the usual channels, to Command Headquarters for which duplicate copies of this letter are attached hereto.

I am,
Sir,
Your obedient servant,

(Sgd) W.G.C.BROWN. Lt.Col.
for Brigadier-General, Director of Personal Services.

The Commandant,
Signal Service Traininf Centre,
WOBURN.

COPY.

OB/7638.

O.C.,
Bedford "B" S.D.

The attached copy of W.O. letter No.121/Drafts etc/7130 (A.G.7) dated 22.10.17 is forwarded for your information and necessary action.

The Officers concerned should be ordered to report to Lieut.A.E.Villiers, R.E.T.C., at 7.10a.m. at Victoria Station on 26.10.17. Each Officer should be furnished with a slip which should be filled in in accordance with Eastern Command Order No.1302 of 1916.

The departure of these Officers should be reported to this Office by wire, quoting the above number.

Lieut.A.E.Villiers should be handed the attached list of Officers who have been ordered to report to him at Victoria Station at 7.10a.m. 26.10.17. This list should then be amended if necessary and disposed of as laid down in E.C.Order No.2129 of 1916.

Please give him also the enclosed letter, with amendments if necessary, to post before leaving Folkestone.

(Sgd) R.BERNARD.
Captain R.Eds.
Brigade Major.

Headquarters,
S.S.T.Centre,
BEDFORD.24.10.17.

Oct 27: Folkestone to Boulonge.

Oct 28: 7.26am train to Abbeville. Stayed at Officers Club. Draft consisted of the following besides myself: Ratcliffe (from S27 class), Randall (S28), Logan (S31), Plowman (S30), Bottwood (S24), Addenbrooke (S30), Villiers (Lt KRR.), Porteous (Lt Scot Rifles). Stayed at Abbeville till Nov 5.

Nov 5: Logan and I detailed to report to 3rd Army HQ. Left Abbeville by 8.30pm (nominally, actually 12.30am) train which took us as far as Romescamp, a derelict junction near nowhere, once a French railhead. Here we had to wait (Nov 6) from 6.30am to 7pm. Logan and I explored the country a little and waded in mud to a so called belvedere near Abancourt (1.5km) which proved a frost. Fortunately the YMCA provide certain shelter at Romescamp plus hot water and food. Eventually set off for Albert, where we arrived 11pm, having taken nearly 24 hours to come about 130 km, to reach a place 50km from Abbeville as the crow flies. Camouflage, I suppose, as the RTOs en route won't tell you the name of your destination. Spent night at Officers Club, Albert.

Nov 7: Reported to 3rd Army Signals at 9.30am. Logan detailed to IVth Corps and I to 12th Division, who I am told (by Col Newbigging, the D Signals, who interviewed us) are at present in rest. I am told a car is going part of the way immediately. Find it, occupied by 1 other sub and journey via Acheux, Doullens and Avesnes-le-Comte to Aubigny. A good lunch here. Many Portuguese strolling about. HQ of 47th Div. From here by a civilian train at 4pm via St Pol to Hesdin. A travelling acquaintance of the ASC knows Leather, who was once his OC Coy, though this man is old enough to be his grandfather. Says Leather now seconded to infantry. Met at Hesdin by 12th Div Signal Co's Sunbeam with the No 1 Sub (d'Andria) and 35th Bde Sig Offr (Gill). Out to the 12 Div HQ, in rest at Wail, 8km out of Hesdin. A hearty welcome from the OC, Major F R Cobb of the Devons, a regular. Others there were Jerome (36th Bde) - was in the RBs of 59th Bde, 20th Div - Smith, also Devons (37th Brigade) and Mathews, Royal Sussex, Wireless. Mess in a farm house. Besides the Sig Coy, the 69th Fields Co were also at Wail. The 35 Bde (7 Norfolks, 7 Suffolks, 9 Essex, 5 Roy Berks, 35 MG Co and 35 Light TMB) were at Vaux, the 36 Bde (8 and 9 RF, 7 Roy Ssx, 11 Msx, 36

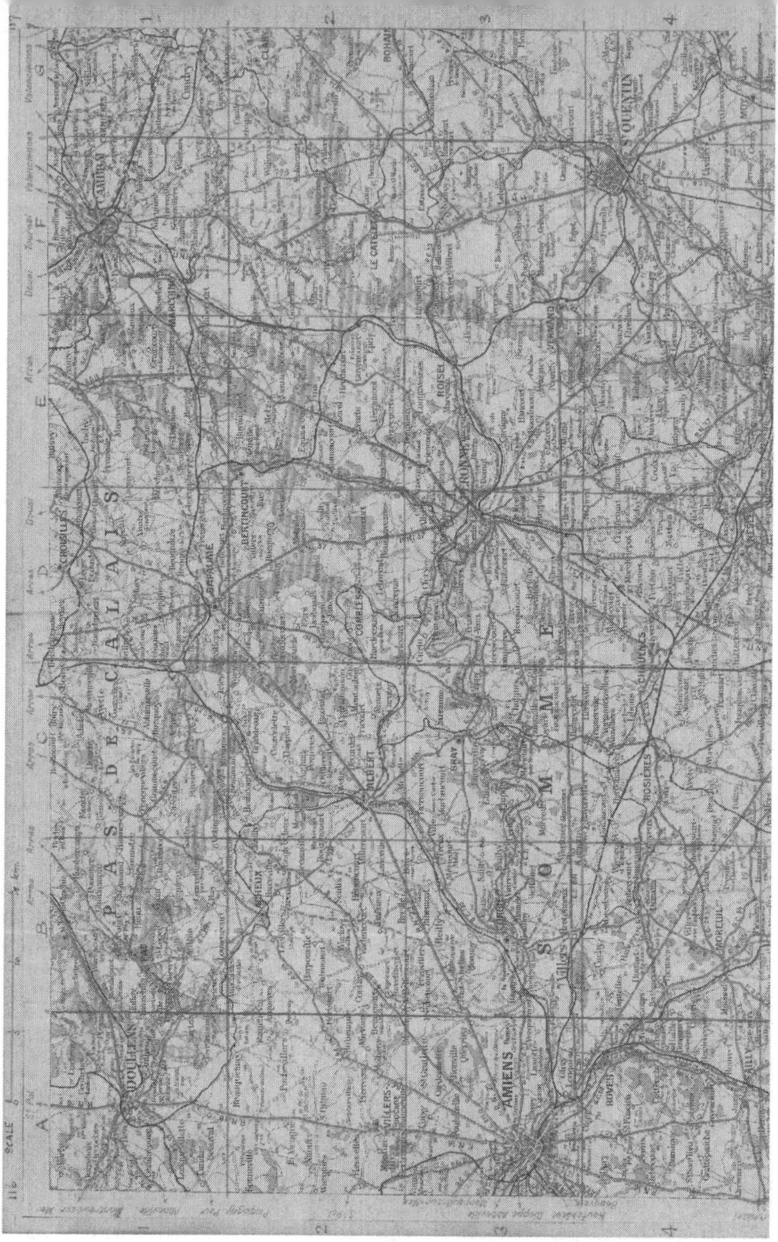

MG Co, 36 L Co TMB) at Willeman, 37 Bde at Beauvoir Chateau (6 The Queens, 6 Buffs, 7 E Surrey, 6 RWK, MG Co & TMB). Other Divisional units round were 235 MG Co, 23 Mob Vet, Div Train, 36, 37 & 38 F Amb. The 5 Northants (Pioneers) and 70th and 87th Field Cos were with the 20th Div. The Divl Arty was still at Arras. Railhead was at Frévent (15km).

Nov 8: At Wail. Am told, in the strictest confidence, of a stunt to come off soon on the Somme front – the 2nd in command (Rice-

Jones) is already down there prospecting. I am to go down there tomorrow with a party of men to him and lay trench lines.

Nov 9: Take Sergeant Baker and 10 sappers by 3-ton lorry via Frévent, Doullens, Albert, Bapaume, le Transloy, Etricourt, to Heudicourt (86km). Pass through the battlefields of last year – Pozières, le Sars, etc. Nothing remaining. Realise that whatever the failings of the British Army it can at least do road construction – quite marvellous, the roads rebuilt. Found Rice-Jones' residence, an Armstrong hut, where live also Miller (from S30 class, now 6th Division) and his 2nd in command Captain Jack. Found the line being held by 20th Division, whose HQ are at Sorel-le Grand 2 miles away. 60th Brigade up same road as ourselves – called there one day and saw Sergeant Joe Ross, Maton and others.

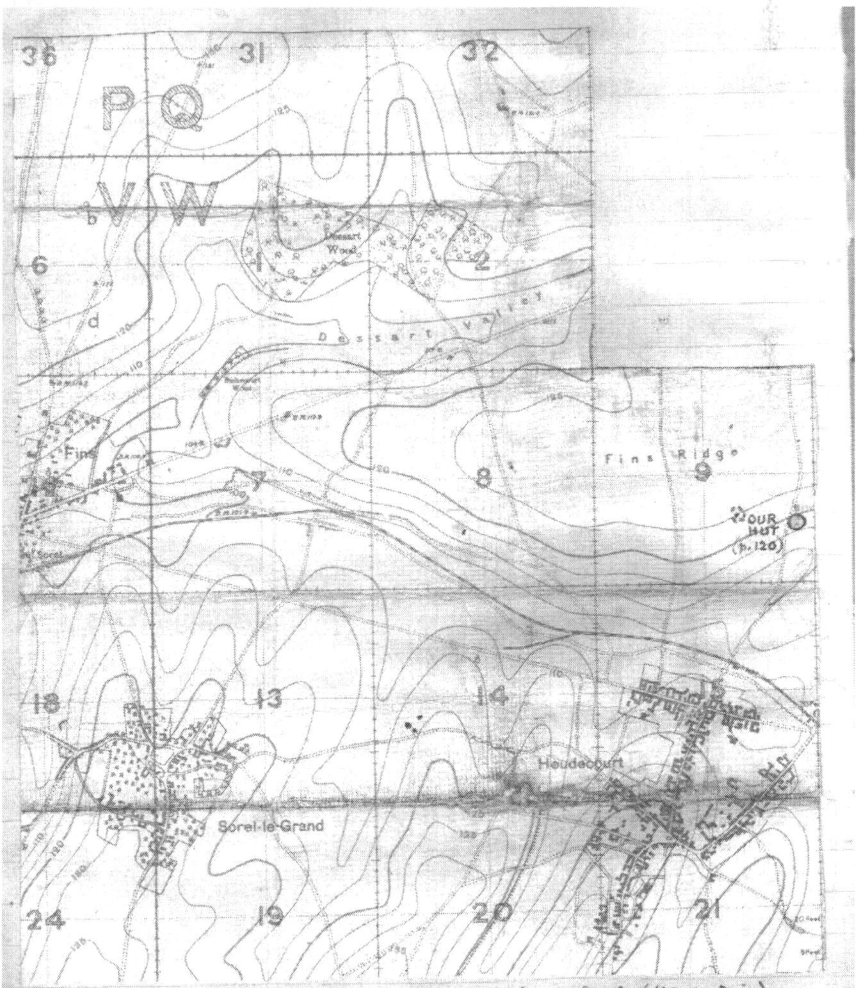

Part of Sheet 57c, shewing Heudecourt (HQ 12 Div) and Sorel (HQ 20 Div). Cf p.122-3

Nov 10: Up the line with RJ (Rice-Jones' usual appellation). Front line runs from east side of Villers Plouich (6th Divisional Front), across Gouzeaucourt-Cambrai road, in front of Gonnelieu, through centre, then bends and to W of Honnecourt (55 Divl Front). 12th Division is apparently to squeeze in also on this front, and our job is to lay a system from end of a multi route from Div (laid by III Corps), tapping Bdes and running to two separate points in front line, to be used as jumping-off points if attack successful. This we did with armoured quad stapled to sides of trenches. No buries allowed for fear of possible listening in by the Boche. The whole thing a mighty secret. I knew, I suppose, as much if not more than the majority of people about, but was forbidden to breathe a word even to officers of the Signal Service. The men of course knew something was coming off. A KOYLI man said they'd been back practisin' a stunt, goin' ower top wi' ranks.

The sappers worked awfully well, though a long march to and from the job. The front very quiet on the whole. MG and rifle fire at night and unhealthy from TMs [trench mortars].

Several buries across roads were necessary and as the Boche had a good view in daylight this meant night work for us. Transport too had to go in the dark, which meant one of us going up to guide wagons and dump stores at night, which after being on one's feet all day made for weariness. Besides the actual carting up and laying of cable, sites for Test Points and material and working parties for their construction, besides numerous other matters had to be arranged.

Curiously, the sub in charge of the corps working party laying the 25 pair lead was Dutton (S27).

Nov 13: Sgt Baker and men took up quarters on the Villers-Guislain-Gonnelieu road in dugouts. After a busy day had a busy night with the transport, starting well by getting ditched at the outset – had to unload every ounce!

Nov 14: Buried 14 pairs (two 7-pair lead-covered) in cable trenches at night. About 2500 yards. A weary march back at 3am, having been up the line since 9am. Found Signal Co and Div arrived.

Nov 17: Jointing and testing through on the right sector, which is all laid. Average of one dis pair on each stretch. Left sector still unfinished, Corporal Stanier's party at it all out.

Nov 19: Stanier's party, having finished testing through, arrive in front line to find considerable section knocked out by shell fire. Worked splendidly and got new piece in by nightfall and tested through. One pair dis.

Evening – busy taking up cable to sap heads and rations for men detailed to occupy test points. The ground alive with tanks crawling up towards the front. Pitch dark. RJ up in the car, working at another point. Eventually (Nov 20) returned together in car at 4.30am. 6.20am Zero hour. None of the guns which had been brought up had fired before this. 365 tanks on Army front went over, followed by infantry. 29th Div (HQ at Quentin Mill) were in reserve. No line through this day (to 37 Bde).

THE BRITISH FRONT NEAR CAMBRAI.

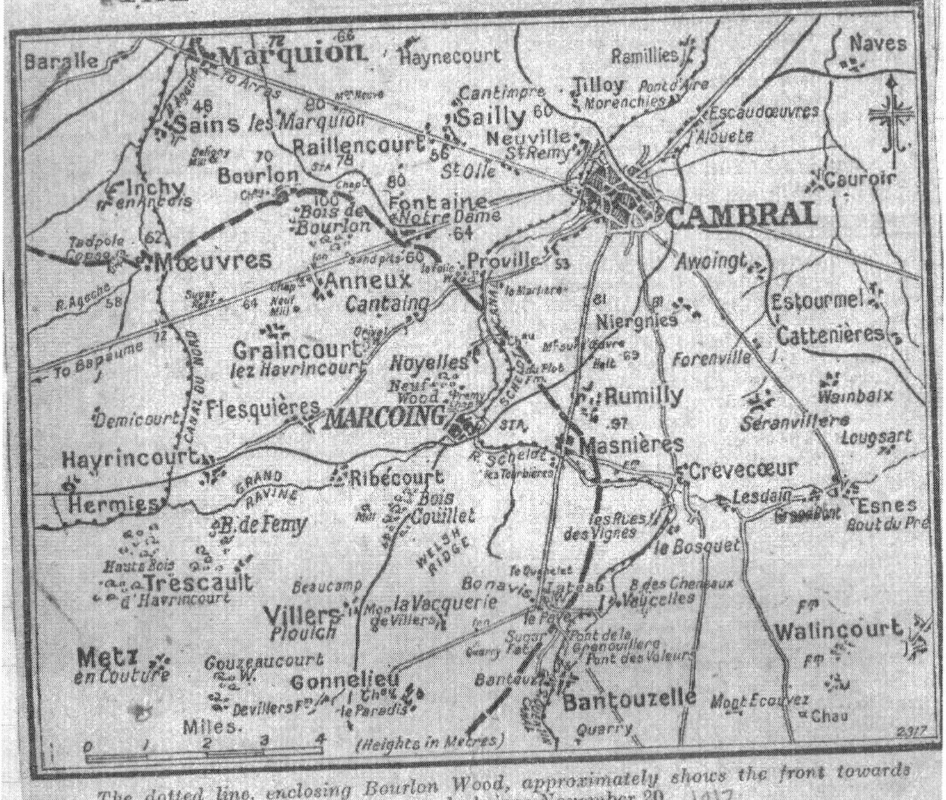

The dotted line, enclosing Bourlon Wood, approximately shows the front towards Cambrai which British troops have reached since November 20. 1917

3 DRs out for many hours trying to find their HQ. RJ reconnoitred ground to a certain extent. 36 Bde had previously moved to Gonnelieu. 35 Brigade remained in Villers Guislain.

Idea was that cavalry should get through gap made initially and reach Cambrai and if possible, hold it, blowing up railways east thereof. Checked, however at the canal at Masnières, where a tank broke down the bridge in crossing. Also northwards at Bourlon Wood, the Boche having apparently just imported a division from Russia, which got to work against us. Cavalry patrols did get to outskirts of Cambrai, which they said the Boche had left. Not strong enough to remain however, and the infantry couldn't get up so far as they were done in. Line eventually formed – Bourlon-Masnières-Lateau Wood- the Boche returning to Rumilly and firing on our troops in Masnières with MGs from the houses.

Nov 21: Up early on horse to Quentin Mill, where I picked up L/Cpl Thompson with men and pack ponies and cable. Sent horse back from Gonnelieu. 'Jumped off' from Left Sap Head and laid out across country to 37 Bde. Greatly hindered by Boche wire and in some measure by his trenches – having to send pack ponies round by road, losing them for a time and running out of cable meanwhile. Pelting rain. Considerable sniping from other side of valley. Some dead, both British and Boche. Came across two field batteries in a hollow firing from the open – a change from the usual camouflaged gun pits. Tanks were parked here too. Line when eventually laid (2.30pm) was found dis. Returned over it and found it cut to bits by a tank in slight hollow of ground. Fairly continuous MG fire from ridge and we had to lie on our backs to joint. Eventually through at 3.30. The 37 Bde were in Boche dugouts where they had taken over an abandoned Hun Signal office complete with instruments and 10 line exchange. Eventually got back, thoroughly wet, to Gonnelieu, where I waited for RJ's arrival in the car, he was going to stay up at Gonnelieu and man a forward exchange (at the Gum Boot Store). Sent party back to Quentin Mill. Found lineman at Gin Avenue TP. OK but confusion in bridging of lines. Osmond and Bingham at Left Sap head had dugout nearly annihilated by a tank, but the lines stuck it. Had dinner with Case, SC 37 Brigade, at their Rear HQ at Gonnelieu. The road from La Vacquerie in the morning was thronged with civilians from Masnières.

Nov 23: Poled an RA line from left Sap head to left Group beyond la Vacquerie. Embarrassed though unsuspected auditor of telephone conversation on very loud instrument between Cobb and RJ about recommendations for decorations. RJ suggested names of various NCOs and men, also me, but OC thought time I'd been with unit too short but said he would send my name to Army for inclusion in their orders.

Nov 24: Continued poling. Found 2 bays down from shell fire. Had to lay about 80 yards slack on ground, as place lousy with batteries. Splendid view through telescope from Left Group of Masnières, Rumilly and Cambrai.

Nov 25: With Ryan (OC 12 Div Arty Sigs) to see various Group Commanders etc.

Nov 26: 35 Bde moved from working post to cross post at Villers Guislain.

Nov 27 Arrival of Vidal to replace me, who am ordered to 24 Div. Remember Vidal as Oi/c Messing at Haynes Park in S27 days. Owing to weak heart hasn't been GS before.

Nov 28: Take Vidal round – Villers Guislain, Gonnelieu, la Vacquerie. Determine some spare pairs for Winder (62 Bde RFA Sig Offr). They are moving to Villers Guislain.

Nov 29: Up at Gouzeaucourt on a line which Cpl Gensavage is laying to 50th HAG from TP at 277 AFA Bde HQ.

Nov 30: The Boche, who had been reported as massing near Banteux, attacked at 7am. Broke through 55 Divl flank at Villers Guislain and took us from both sides. 35 Bde HQ surprised. Gill (Sig Offr 35 Bde) rushed down to Heudicourt half clad and gave us the news. Boche eventually checked at Vancelette Farm. Div HQ prepare to move to Sorel. I go out to find some existing pair thither. Cable wagon lays one as well. Then up along the 25 pair lead-covered with a driver, on a horse and a mule respectively, all that is left in the stables, to cut it forward in case of leakage. Tanks being brought up. Considerable rifle and MG fire and we discover we are at the front line. See the Boche ahead. We retire a couple of hundred yards and cut the lines. Meet Ryan, who wants a line laid to 35th at Revelon Farm. Return to collect some men and cable and lay it. Most of the Hun shelling centred on Revelon Farm and to the north of it. Cavalry are up and go over, only to be held up by the wire. Return and go up to Gouzeaucourt. Anxious as to fate of RJ, who was with 30 sappers at Gonnelieu Forward Exchange. Some straggle in, but know nothing of him. Very little news, so we can't tell where people are. Divl HQ move at 6pm to Sorel. I am left in charge at Heudicourt with about 70 of the Signal Co and attached men, to run it as a forward exchange. Hear RJ is safe and has done jolly well.

More Signals struggle in every now and then. 35 Bde holds the line in front of us with a composite battalion of 500 – all sorts and sizes. The Yank light railway people at Gouzeaucourt fought jolly well this am. Ryan stops the night at Heudicourt. Bde of 21 Div comes into Heudicourt (64th). Gill has lost all his private kit, all signal stores gone west, 1 sergeant wounded. Signal Co casualties Nov 30 - Killed 1 NCO, 2 sappers. Wounded 2 NCOs, 2 or 3 sappers. Missing Lt Winder (62 RFA subsection) reported later prisoner – 1 sapper.

Dec 2: To Sorel in vain search for lost small kit.

Dec 3: Cpl Stanier arrived with cable wagon from Divn (who have moved to Liéramont). Lay line to 35 Bde HQ from HQ of composite battalion at Vancelette Farm. In afternoon get orders to lay line with cable wagon from 35 Bde to Guards Bde on left, location not very definitely known. Lay up road, thence across country. Find them eventually. By laying at the trot we just finished laying by dusk. Met Maj Clarke, OC Sigs 61 Divn, one time subaltern in the 20th. Line through. 36 and 37 Bdes come to Heudicourt. Jerome looks very done, though Smith had a more exciting time I fancy.

Dec 4: Tee line to NRC (63 RFA) at Queen's Cross. Dutton to supper with me at Heudicourt.

Dec 5: Fetched by Maj Bollam, OC 24 Sig Co per Ford car. Called at Liéramont to say goodbye to 12th. YX HQ at Nobescourt Farm, near Roisel.

Dec 6: 24th Division Nobescourt Farm
Left Brigade, 73rd Sig Offr Ballantyne
9 Sussex, 7 Northants, 13 Middlesex, 2 Lenisters, 73 MG Co
also 6th & 14th KB Sections, 103 Field Co RE

Central Brigade 72nd Hervilly, Sig Offr Hopkinson
8 RW Surrey, 9 E Surrey, 8 RWK, 1 N Staffs
Right Brigade 17th Sig Offr Fowler
8 E Kents, 1 RF, 12 RF, 3 RB
Right Group Artillery

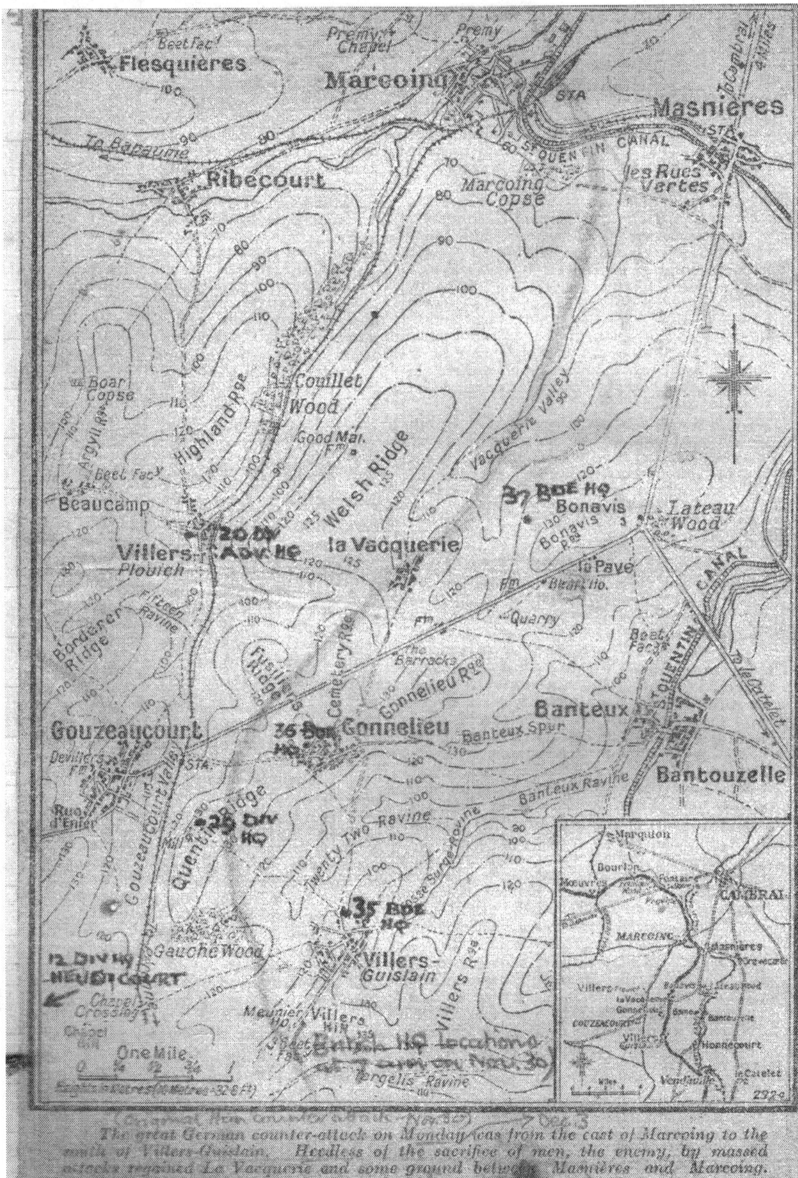

(Ground lost in counter attack Nov 30 → Dec 3)

The great German counter-attack on Monday was from the east of Marcoing to the south of Villers-Guislain. Heedless of the sacrifice of men, the enemy, by massed attacks regained La Vacquerie and some ground between Masnières and Marcoing. They had exceptionally heavy losses on the high ground north of La Vacquerie.

Left Group Artillery
106 & 107 RFA
Other Units 12 Sherwoods (Pioneers) 191 MG Co, 36 Mob Vet, 103, 104 & 129 Field Cos RE, V,X, Y, Z/24 Heavy TMBs, 72, 73, 74 Field Ambulances

Divisional lines largely semi-permanent routes.
Test Points: Rouilles Wood, Bernes, Hervilly (Centre Bde), Smallfoot Wood (Right Bde)
Wireless/Telegraphy Stations: Hargicourt Quarry, Cooker's Quarry
PB Stations: 'Bower Lane', Btn HQ Hargicourt (PB & Amp)

Dec 12: By road (car) to Amiens, together with the senior Padre, Camp Commandant (going on leave) and Jackson of the Northants. Stayed at Hotel de l'Univers.

Dec 13: Lunched at Goberts. Visited cathedral in afternoon. Return by car to Nobescourt Farm.

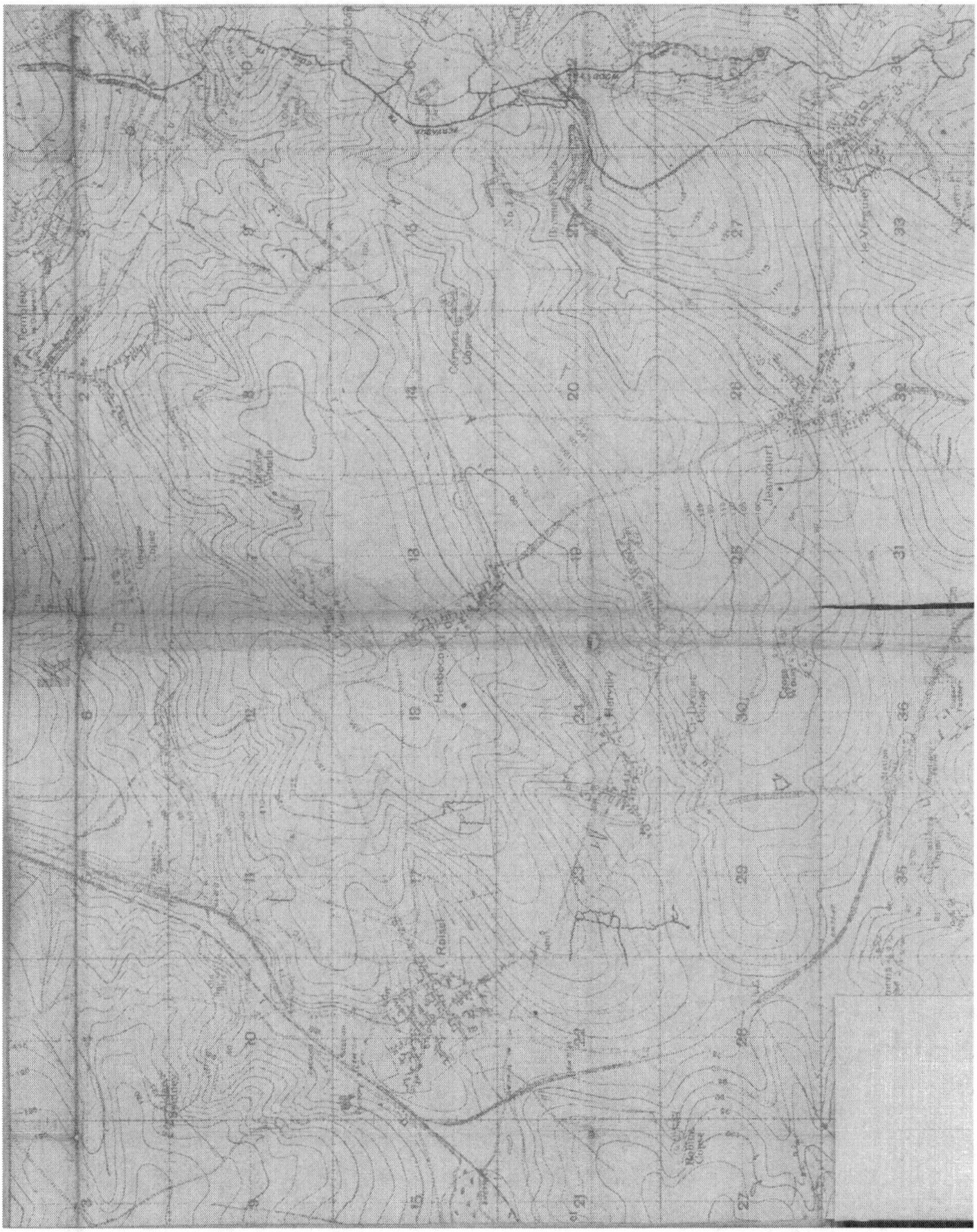

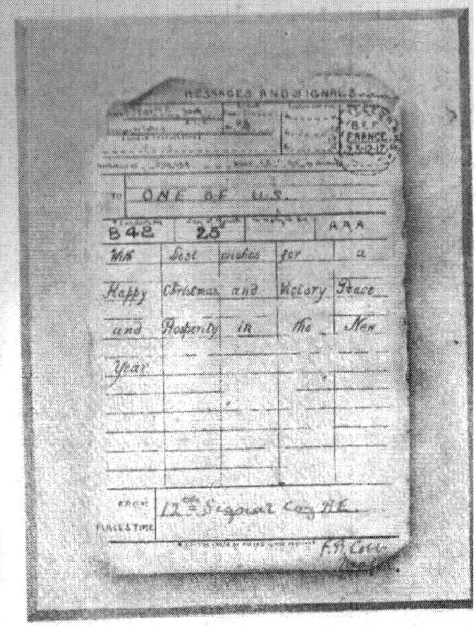

MESSAGES AND SIGNALS

B.E.F. FRANCE 23.12.17

To ONE OF US.

842 25 AAA

With best wishes for a Happy Christmas and Victory Peace and Prosperity in the New Year

From 12th Signal Coy R.E.

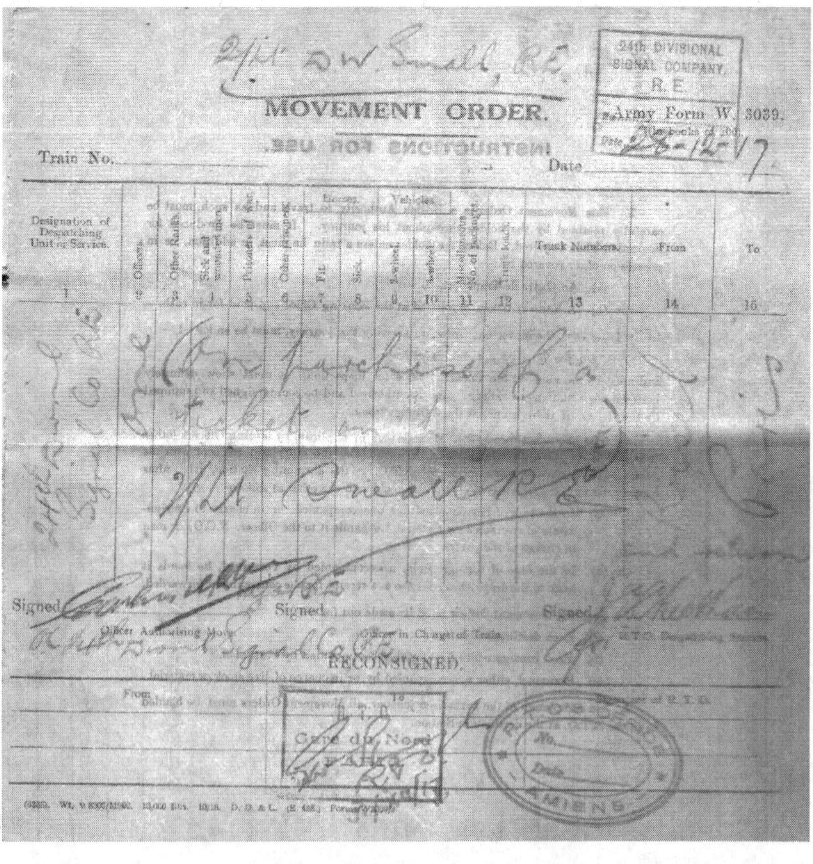

2/Lt D.W. Small, R.E.

24th DIVISIONAL SIGNAL COMPANY, R.E.

MOVEMENT ORDER.

Army Form W. 3039.

Date 23-12-17

Train No. Date

Designation of Despatching Unit or Service.	Officers.	Other Ranks.	Sick and wounded	Prisoners of War	Other passengers	Horses Fit	Horses Sick	Vehicles 2-wheeled	Vehicles 4-wheeled	Miscellaneous No. of Packages	Truck load	Truck Numbers	From	To
1	2	3	4	5	6	7	8	9	10	11	12	13	14	15
24th Divl Signal Co RE	On purchase of a ticket only													
	2/Lt D Small RE													

Signed ... Officer Authorising Move. 24th Divl Signal Co RE

Signed ... Officer in Charge of Train.

Signed ... R.T.O. Despatching Station

RECONSIGNED.

From To

R.T.O. Gare du Nord PARIS

R.T.O. AMIENS

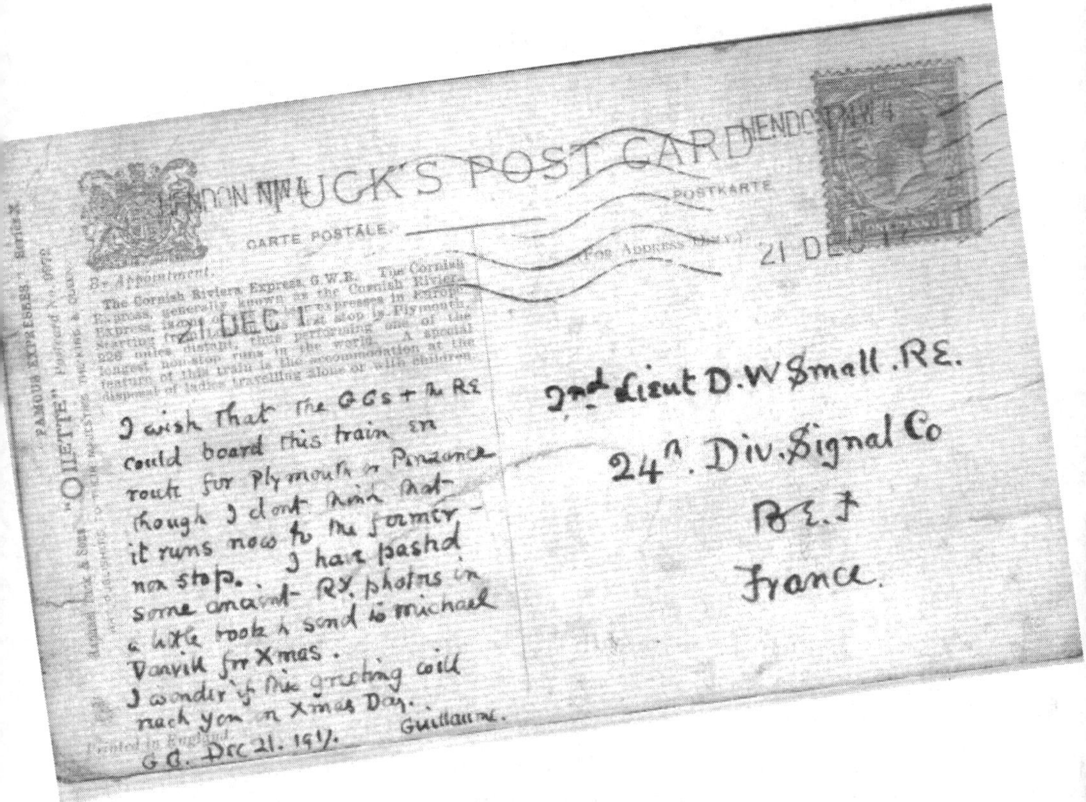

Dec 28: Got Paris leave. Left Nobescourt Farm in Ford car about 8 for Roisel, thence train which took all day to get to Amiens, arrived too late to get on to Paris. Stopped at Hotel de l'Univers.

Dec 29: On to Paris. Stayed with Cobb at his brother's, who lives in Paris. In evening to see Gaby Deslys at Casino de Paris.

Dec 30: To Notre Dame, les Invalides, etc.

Dec 31: Left Paris for 24 Division again. Spent night at officers club at Péronne.

1918

Jan 1 Péronne to Roisel in early morning. Part of the way in the '*vigie*' [observation point] of a goods van. Back to Nobescourt Farm.

Jan 4: Relieve Ballantyne at 73rd Bde as Bde Signal Offr while he goes on leave. Brigade in support at Bernes.

Jan 8: Brigade move to Vraignes, in reserve.

Jan 21: Brigade move into the line at Hautwood, near Templeux-le-Guérard.

Jan 26: Back to Division.

Jan 26 – Feb 20: In charge of Divisional Wireless vice Ritchie, who is away on a course at Abbeville.

Mar 2: 24th Div holding a 3-bridgade front from NE of Hargicourt to S of le Verguier, relieved in the line by 66 Div. Original project was to go back to the Corbie area for a months training but this was cancelled and Div HQ move to Méréaucourt.

Mar 6: OC Sigs (Bollam) to England on a months leave. OC DA Sigs (Pelham-Clinton) becomes acting OC Coy and I go to DA, at Monchy-Lagache, separated from Méréaucourt by the river Omignon.

Mar 9: Our forthcoming relief of Cav Dismounted Div in the line from le Verguier to Vermand is precipitated by prisoners' statements that Boche attacking next day. Div HQ move to Bouvincourt at midnight.

Mar 11: Div Arty HQ move to Bouvincourt. Left Group (311 AFA Bde) HQ at Vendelles. Sub-group HQ in railway cutting at Vendelles. Right Group (107 Bde) HQ at Vermand. Sub group, Royal Canadian HA Bde.

Mar 20: Again prisoners declare Boche attack to be made at dawn on 21st, with 10 hrs bombardment.

Mar 21: Dawn. Boche attacks heavily on front extending from Gouzeaucourt to La Fère. Vendelles and Vermand HQ heavily shelled with much gas. Back area shelling – Estrées aerodrome, Bouvincourt, Tincourt. This did not start till later in the morning. Communication to both groups holds. Civilians evacuated from Bouvincourt in afternoon. Maissemy captured by Boche in pm. Story, Sig Offr of 107 Bde, wounded in morning. In afternoon, a reinforcement from 19 Corps in his place, Tait (S31). He hangs on at DA for the barrage on Vermand road to die down. Duplicate command lines into old Boche sap below road outside HQ. At 5pm, another sub is sent from Corps in place of Tait. Take him up to Vermand in Corps car. Still plastering Vermand. Find only adjutant and a few signals of 107 still there, remainder seeking a new HQ with colonel. Leave the subaltern, load up car with wireless operators and apparatus and seek their new HQ. Find them in the middle of a field E of Poeuilly, just in rear of batteries, together with the Canadian HA (Col Elkins). Communication by a D3 on a tee to the main route, which still held.

Sgt Wright i/c Signals, doing wonders. Only means of communication to batteries by Lucas lamp and runners. Return to Bouvincourt and send Tait back to Corps.

Shell hits Div Signal Office and kills 5, wounding 2. Brunt of attack slacks off in early afternoon and again at night.

Mar 22: Fresh attack at dawn. Takes le Verguier and penetrates on left flank divisional front (66th) as far as Roisel, later gaining Jeancourt and then Hervilly. Also penetrates right flank division (61st). Bouvincourt again shelled. Vermand taken during morning,

Right Group have HQ near Poeuilly. Left Group evacuate Vendelles and withdraw to Fléchin.

New HQ selected for DA at St Cren (Mons-en-Chaussée). Div HQ have already moved back to Brie and promise to send a cable detachment to St Cren to lay tee to main route, so that we may have communication to groups, but wrong directions delay it. Send all men to St Cren except office staff and linemen and DRs and ultimately go down there per Triumph to see what has happened. Roads crowded with every conceivable sort of traffic flowing backwards. As I leave he has started again on Bouvincourt and when I get back is shelling it heavily. Find one of the DRs suffering from shock – blown off his bike, but he pulls together and we ride across country into the back of the village. The 311th Bde has already come in earlier in the afternoon. The Boche at this time (7pm) somewhere about Poeuilly. Tell Bde Major (Richardson) that we should have communication at any rate as far as Estrées by the time St Cren reached. (There was a Divl Test at Estrées.) But can't tell when the permanent routes mayn't go down. Clear out of Bouvincourt with some difficulty. Air bursts all down the main road to just E of Mons-en-Chaussée, but not many casualties to transport on the road. At St Cren we get communication by wire to 50th DA (at le Mesnil Bruntel) from where our CRA(Gen Nairne) is directing combined DAs of 24, 50, 66 and 8 Divns; also to Right Grp in Mons. Left Grp with DA. A brigade (149 Inf Brigade) of 50th Division in St Cren. These are the first reinforcements to arrive and 24 Division is ordered to retire fighting through the 50th Div.

Mar 23: At about 3am the 24th DA get orders to cover the sector from Mons-en-Chaussée southwards to south of Gouzeaucourt, while the divisions in that area withdraw over the Somme. Move off at daybreak. Disposition, north to south: 311, 106, 251 AFA Brigade, RCHA, 107. Establish a system of Report Centres for communication but very little use made of them: 2 motorcyclists at 150 Inf Bde (50th Div), Athies, 3 push cyclists and a mounted DR at the Cimetière, St Christ, working back to Div HQ at Marchélepot. Remainder of Signal Section under Sgt Marshall sent back to Marchélepot. Fail to find acting CRA (Colonel Spiller) or Bde Major in Athies, so go down per Triumph to St Christ to see if party arrived. St Christ bridge being got ready for blowing up.

Return to Athies and eventually meet BM and CRA with 251 Bde. They were in communication by flag with Canadian HA who were being shrapnelled but not heavily. I had previously met Major Welsh bringing 106 Bde through Athies on their way down to St Christ. He told me that as far as he knew they were the last of the Left Group to leave. Right Group therefore commenced to fall back.

Then to St Christ, where no shelling of bridges had occurred. Then back to Marchélepot to arrange if possible communication with the groups when they have taken up their new positions W of the canal. Found Marchélepot almost impassable – 24th Div HQ, 2 CCS, one road filled with double-banked lorries, various divisions' troops passing through, among them the 8th Div Sig Co. Found remainder of section and HQ with Roffey (Reconnaissance Officer). Find Division on point of moving back to Hallu. No sooner does one get within reach of the Signal Coy than before one has time to ask them for anything they dash away again. Have no cable at all, so lines out of the question. Returning towards St Christ, find RCHA near Licourt, but still on the move. Eventually DA HQ established in old PoW camp on Chaulnes-Omiécourt road. Left Group HQ at Misery, Right Group at Pertain. Cable detachment again promised by division but partly owing to wrong directions and partly to Lord knows what, they didn't turn up till 1am.

About 7 of the sisters and patients from the Marchélepot Casualty Clearing Stations went past towards Chaulnes. About 8 go in to Div by car with the Bde Major. Secured some DIIIs and Lucas Lamps. At 1am L/Cpl Spackman turned up with the detachment, having laid a line from Corps Test at Chaulnes. Sent him on laying at Right Group at Pertain. Boche reported over the canal. One of the southern bridges said not to have been blown up properly. Get 4 hours sleep.

Mar 24: Detachment out at 6am laying tee from Pertain line to Left Group. HQ transport and Signal Section not on duty sent back to Caix, 7 miles SE of Villers Bretonneux. Col Stirling RHA acting CRA. Boche gradually advancing this side of canal, but the strafe slacked off in afternoon. Rumours current that Ostend, Lille and Lens in our hands with 25,000 prisoners. Wonder who is the sot who starts these things. Apropos of rumours, some Boche gents in

British uniforms – one as a Signal officer – create a panic among the transport by reporting the Uhlans to have broken through about dusk. Some rifles fired off at Rosières completes their success. My transport (I had gone down that way to bring back reliefs and kits, as CRA decided to stop another night there) got caught up in the stream, eventually managing to get back to DA about 1.30am.

Mar 25: Boche reported advancing on Marchélepot and Dreslincourt. Omiécourt being regularly shelled all the time. Right Group have dropped back there from Pertain. Go out with one of my DRs and salve a 4-horse Douglas and sidecar which was stranded without a carburettor needle. It proves very useful. MG fire in front very heavy. Fache, the Signal Offr of RCHA, turns up, weary but cheerful, with a view of taking over our lines when we move back and they take our place.

About 11am Divisional Artillery moves back to Lihons. Lay a tee to a permanent route and get communication to Chaulnes Test and thus to Division, who are at Rosières. Chaulnes Test manned by 8th Div Signals. The Boche in Omiécourt and Marchélepot. Right Group comes back to Chaulnes and gets communication with us by enamelled wire. Left Group more or less in the blue. Get an order that no further retirement is to be made by the Division from Chaulnes-Hattencourt line. Go down to Division to try for more cable. About 6pm DA moves back to Rosières, where quite a busy exchange is still being manned by Div men. Boche planes over dropping bombs – almost the first I'd seen by day since the show started. Sprain ankle getting off horse and become useless for work. 'Passengers' no use to HQ at this juncture so ignominiously retire in sidecar to Field Ambulance.

Mar 26: Moved from 72 FA at Cayeux to 41 Stationary Hospital at Cerisy – here they are just evacuating – MG fire very loud just in front, get taken on and eventually land in 42 Stat Hosp Amiens. Spend about 6 hours here, it is absolutely crowded. Boche planes play havoc with the town from 8pm onwards. Am eventually put on a motor road convoy to No 2 Stat Hosp, Abbeville, arrive about 3am.

Apr 9: Discharged from hospital and report to Signal Depot Abbeville.

Apr 10: By car from Abbeville to St Valery, where 24 Division have gone back to refit, etc. Rejoin Div HQ.

Apr 14: By road to Sorel (16km SE of Abbeville) to be Signal Officer of 106 RFA Bde Signal Sub-Section.

Apr 17: Brigade march to Bellancourt (6km E of Abbeville).

Apr 18: March route via Bussus and Domléger to Beauvois Rivière, 2 miles SE of Auxi-le-Chateau.

Apr 19: March route by Frévent and St Pol to Hernicourt.

Apr 21: March route by St Pol, Buneville and Houvin to Estrée-Wamin.

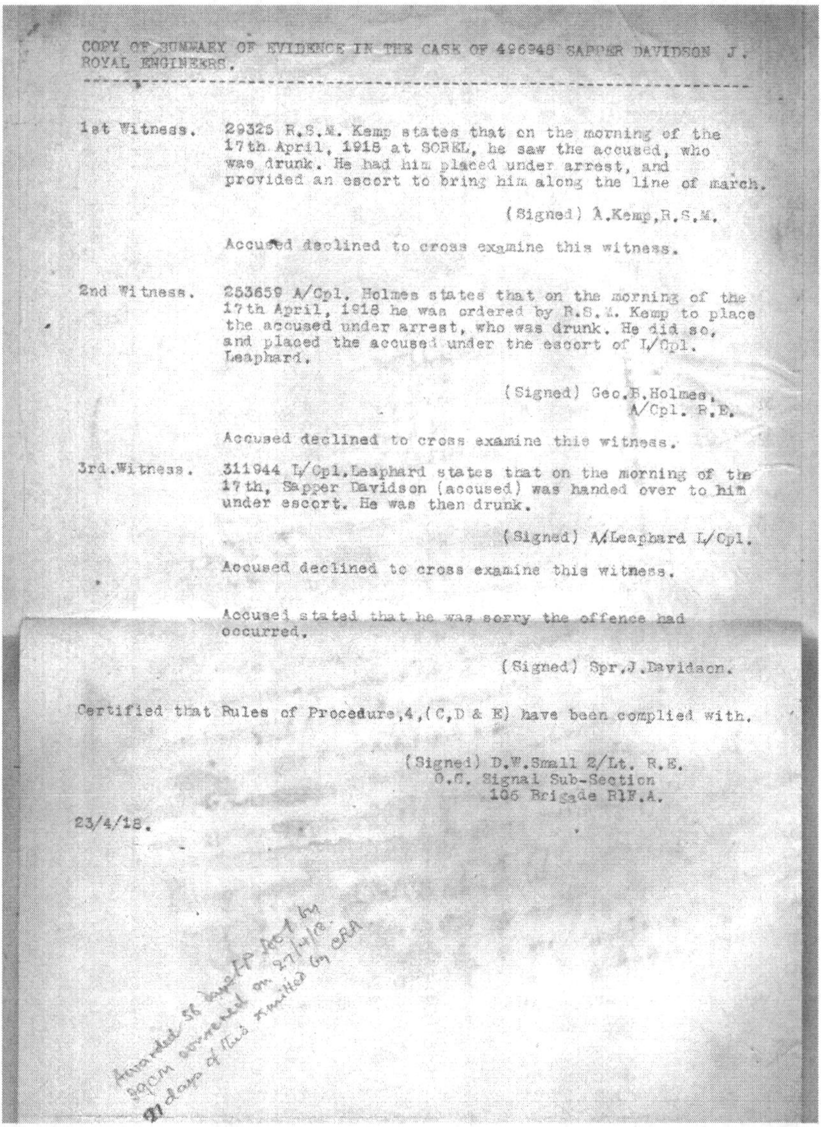

COPY OF SUMMARY OF EVIDENCE IN THE CASE OF 496948 SAPPER DAVIDSON J. ROYAL ENGINEERS.

1st Witness. 29325 R.S.M. Kemp states that on the morning of the 17th April, 1918 at SOREL, he saw the accused, who was drunk. He had him placed under arrest, and provided an escort to bring him along the line of march.

(Signed) A.Kemp,R.S.M.

Accused declined to cross examine this witness.

2nd Witness. 253659 A/Cpl. Holmes states that on the morning of the 17th April, 1918 he was ordered by R.S.M. Kemp to place the accused under arrest, who was drunk. He did so, and placed the accused under the escort of L/Cpl. Leaphard.

(Signed) Geo.E.Holmes,
A/Cpl. R.E.

Accused declined to cross examine this witness.

3rd.Witness. 311944 L/Cpl.Leaphard states that on the morning of the 17th, Sapper Davidson (accused) was handed over to him under escort. He was then drunk.

(Signed) A/Leaphard L/Cpl.

Accused declined to cross examine this witness.

Accused stated that he was sorry the offence had occurred.

(Signed) Spr.J.Davidson.

Certified that Rules of Procedure,4,(C,D & E) have been complied with.

(Signed) D.W.Small 2/Lt. R.E.
O.C. Signal Sub-Section
106 Brigade RlF.A.

23/4/18.

Awarded 56 days F.P. No 1 by FGCM convened on 27/4/18. 21 days of this remitted by CRA

Extract from letter home written from Estrée-Wamin:

May 1 "… still in the same place though our sojourn is close at an end. T'other day I went into the little town (Frévent) 7 kilometres down the main road in search of one or two *objets de toilette*, walked half the way and jumped a lorry the other half. The *Societé Economique*, whose line follows the road, not being suitable in the matter of a train. But it's a poky little place and I very soon egressed on another lorry back again. Today damp but I had a particularly jolly ride this afternoon with the doctor (Mortimer) through some wooded country about a couple of miles distant. All sorts of familiar friends whom one hadn't seen for full many a year – lesser celandine, wood anemone, viola arvensis, caltha palustris, cowslip, ranunculus arvensis, hawthorn and wonderful vistæ of spring greenery camouflaging tall trunks …

Yours till a labour corps private salutes, DWS"

From letter home May 2 from Estrée Wamin "… our sojourn in this *endroit* is just finishing. It has been a very pleasant one and the powers that be have been gracious in leaving us in one spot for as long as ten days. Quite a country holiday and with the help of my NCOs I've succeeded in getting quite a fair groundwork of battery signalling into my beginners class – most of them proved very keen and some of them can already read at 6 to 7 words a minute. *Par bonheur* we've had very few really wet days. Yesterday was quite an interesting day – certain officers, including Brigade Signal Officers, having assembled at a rendezvous (le Cauroy) not very far away, whither we proceeded at an early hour *à cheval*, installed themselves in a vehicle at one time belonging to the LGOC, but now WD and of more sombre hue. Being a jolly fine day we occupied the top and the 'conductor', a private in the ASC, having rung the bell, we moved off and had a slow but very pleasant journey of about 28 miles, through one or two small towns, one of which (Aubigny) I'd spent a few hours in last year. The object in view was to reconnoitre the area where we shall soon be. We were met by guides and having split up to our various future headquarters and been given lunch by the present tenants, I discoursed with their SO and then went round some of the area (Lens district). We are lucky, at present it is a quiet one, as good as to be found anywhere just now I think. At 4 we returned to our bus and came back. The voyage was rather perilous in that a vigorous alert had to be kept for branches of trees and wires and cables across the road, which often compelled us to lie flat on the top. Needless to say, the Signal Officer had his leg badly pulled about the last named obstacles. This afternoon I had no class and took a holiday, went for a ride with the medicine man….. Truly the country is just at its best and those woods are incomparable. Now I must shut up and bid you goodnight. There are distinct advantages in the places we are going to – rhubarb and gooseberries can be picked in the vicinity and there should be no lack of coal for fuel. I was surprised to see civilians nearly all the way…."

May 4: HQ by lorry via Avesnes-le-Comte, Aubigny, Cambligneul, Sains-en-Gohelle, to near Maroc (Fosse 11 de Béthune). Relieve 242 AFA Bde. Transport by march route to Sains-en-Gohelle.

May 30: (from letter written from HQ 106 brigade RFA) ".. Here we jog along as usual, though I see there is more doing elsewhere. The last few days have been really quite to be enjoyed in spite of all circumstances – bright sunshine, very clear atmosphere with excellent view from our location of land Gallic and Teuton and ground gay with floral colour. A tremendous difference from the '*couleur de boue*' monotone of the Somme region where I was all last winter, though I suppose even that might blossom out under the influence of spring. The predominant elements here are scarlet poppy, yellow hawkweed and white ox-eye daisies…"

June 13: (from letter home, written from Maroc) "I have just got in after a day's wandering round our battery positions etc and found your letter of June 8 to welcome me on my return… We miss a gramophone in this mess – twice recently however I've been down to visit our wagon lines which are in the same place as the Div Signal Coy, whose mess I accordingly visited and played some old friends on theirs, including Debussy's Arabesque, a charming thing… I have just moved into a new billet. I may have told you that we shifted our headquarters a short distance not long ago and the accommodation here was not so good as in the old place. So sundry of my section (among whom is an excellent carpenter) have been converting a couple of cellars into quite passable apartments for your 'umble and the Orderly Officer (Stuart). They are knocked into one and strutted with wood beams within, whitewashed with a mixture of chalk, soap and water (quite effectual!) and are nice and light for working and having two entrances airy also. A big table affords room for sundry maps and diagrams as well as the other litter which a Sig Offr accumulates. I am infinitely superior to you in always having a telephone on my table by day and by my bed at night. The devil of a luxury not always appreciated!

June 24: Got leave to England. Got 'flu while on leave and had extension till July 14.

Aug 26: OR Dinner at St Pol (Hotel de France). About a dozen including from our Divn LJ Clarke, my immediate superior (OC 24 DA Sigs); and PT Chevallier, Bde Major 73rd Infy Bde whom we took home very happy at the finish. There were also HS Altham, WT Greswell, FM Twigg (killed a month later) RL Holdsworth, HM Hall, HW Pasteur, etc.

IRVING THEATRE

CHATEAU DE LA HAIE

SATURDAY 10th August 1918

At 5.30 p.m.

GRAND VAUDEVILLE ENTERTAINMENT

By the combined Concert Parties of the

SEE TOOS, SNIPERS, VER(E)Y LIGHTS

and VOLATILES.

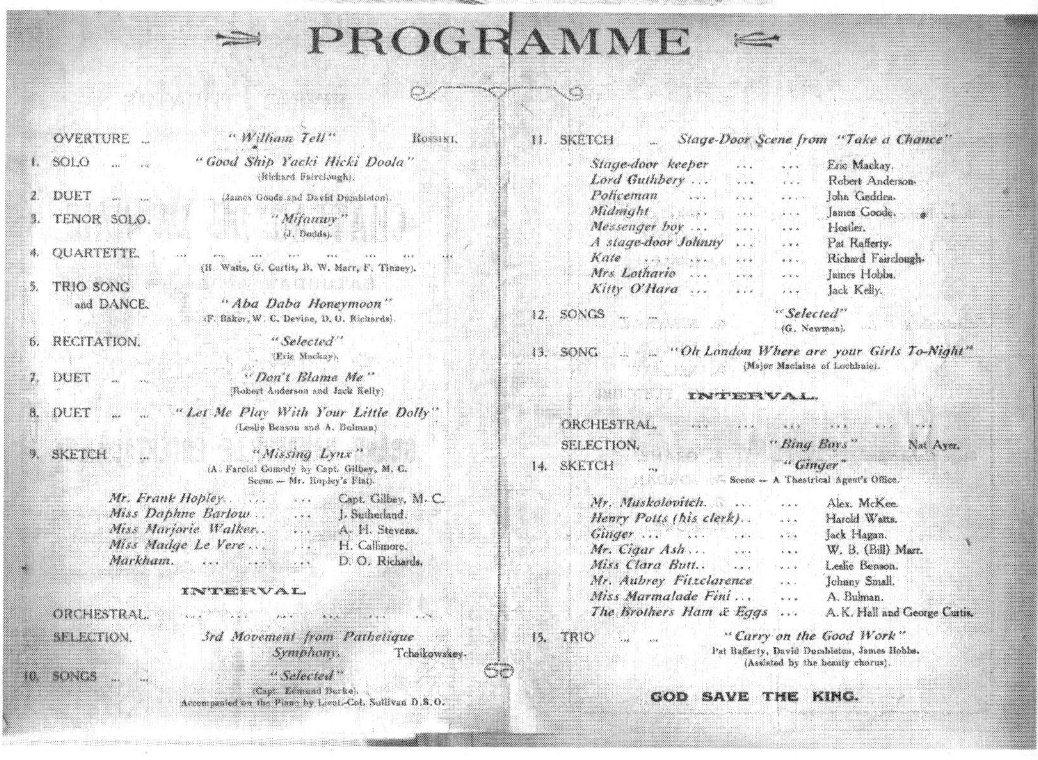

PROGRAMME

OVERTURE ... "*William Tell*" ROSSINI.

1. SOLO ... ... "*Good Ship Yacki Hicki Doola*"
(Richard Fairclough).

2. DUET ... ... (James Goode and David Dumbleton).

3. TENOR SOLO. "*Mifanwy*"
(J. Dodds).

4. QUARTETTE. ... ...
(H. Watts, G. Curtis, B. W. Marr, F. Tinney).

5. TRIO SONG and DANCE. "*Aba Daba Honeymoon*"
(F. Baker, W. C. Devine, D. O. Richards).

6. RECITATION. "*Selected*"
(Eric Mackay).

7. DUET ... ... "*Don't Blame Me*"
(Robert Anderson and Jack Kelly)

8. DUET ... ... "*Let Me Play With Your Little Dolly*"
(Leslie Benson and A. Bulman)

9. SKETCH ... "*Missing Lynx*"
(A. Farcial Comedy by Capt. Gilbey, M. C.
Scene — Mr. Hopley's Flat).

Mr. Frank Hopley ... ... Capt. Gilbey, M. C.
Miss Daphne Barlow ... ... J. Sutherland.
Miss Marjorie Walker ... ... A. H. Stevens.
Miss Madge Le Vere ... ... H. Callimore.
Markham. ... ... D. O. Richards.

INTERVAL.

ORCHESTRAL. ... ...
SELECTION. *3rd Movement from Pathetique Symphony.* Tchaikowskey.

10. SONGS ... ... "*Selected*"
(Capt. Edmund Burke).
Accompanied on the Piano by Lieut.-Col. Sullivan D.S.O.

11. SKETCH ... *Stage-Door Scene from "Take a Chance"*

Stage-door keeper ... ... Eric Mackay.
Lord Guthbery ... ... Robert Anderson.
Policeman ... ... John Geddes.
Midnight ... ... James Goode.
Messenger boy ... ... Hostler.
A stage-door Johnny ... ... Pat Rafferty.
Kate ... ... Richard Fairclough.
Mrs Lothario ... ... James Hobbs.
Kitty O'Hara ... ... Jack Kelly.

12. SONGS ... ... "*Selected*"
(G. Newman).

13. SONG ... ... "*Oh London Where are your Girls To-Night*"
(Major Maclaine of Lochbuie).

INTERVAL.

ORCHESTRAL. ... ...
SELECTION. "*Bing Boys*" Nat Ayer.

14. SKETCH ... "*Ginger*"
Scene — A Theatrical Agent's Office.

Mr. Muskolovitch. ... ... Alex. McKee.
Henry Potts (his clerk) ... ... Harold Watts.
Ginger ... ... Jack Hagan.
Mr. Cigar Ash ... ... W. B. (Bill) Marr.
Miss Clara Butt ... ... Leslie Benson.
Mr. Aubrey Fitzclarence ... Johnny Small.
Miss Marmalade Fini ... ... A. Bulman.
The Brothers Ham & Eggs ... A. K. Hall and George Curtis.

15. TRIO ... ... "*Carry on the Good Work*"
Pat Rafferty, David Dumbleton, James Hobbs.
(Assisted by the beauty chorus).

GOD SAVE THE KING.

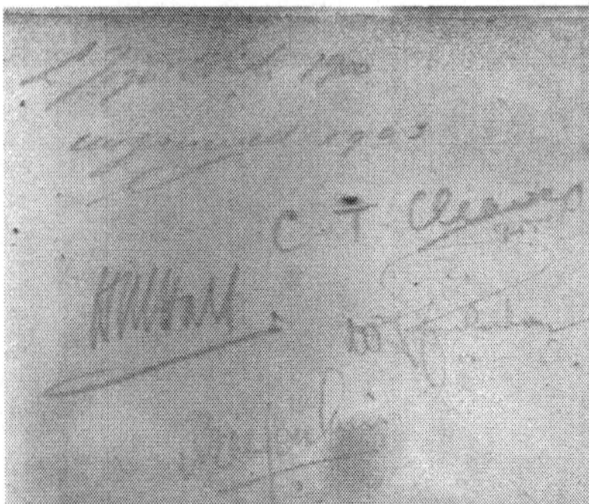

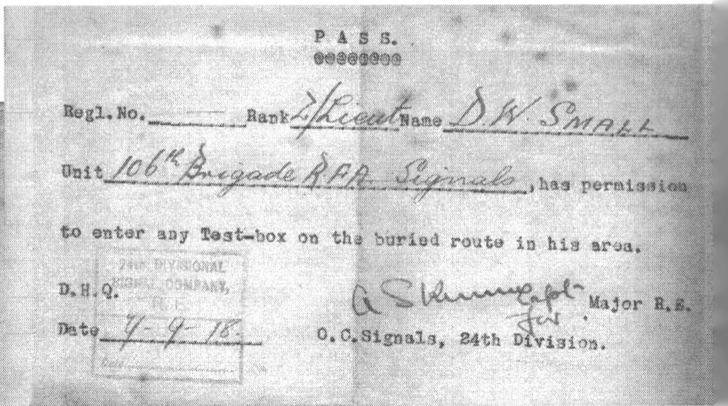

PASS.

Regl. No. ________ Rank 2/Lieut Name D. W. SMALL

Unit 106th Brigade R.F.A. Signals, has permission

to enter any Test-box on the buried route in his area.

D.H.Q.

Date 7-9-18.

Capt. for Major R.E.

O.C. Signals, 24th Division.

24th DIVISIONAL SIGNAL COMPANY, R.E.

OLD REPTONIAN DINNER.

HOTEL DE FRANCE ST. POL

MONDAY 26th AUG. 1918.

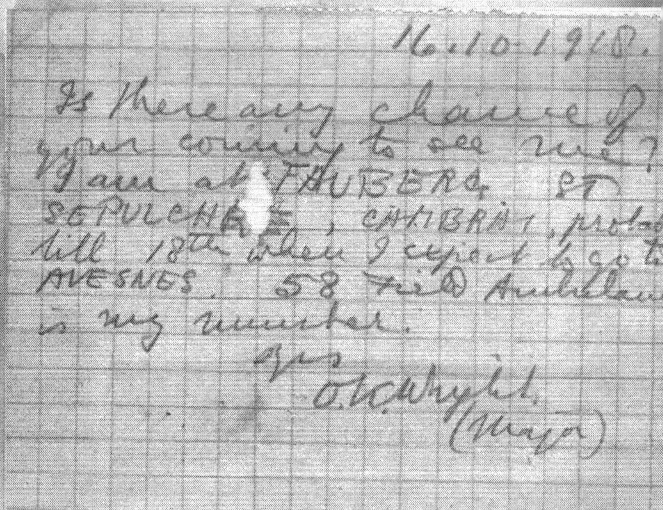

16.10.1918.

Is there any chance of your coming to see me? I am at FAUBERG ST SEPULCHRE, CAMBRAI, prob. till 18th when I expect to go to AVESNES. 58 Field Ambulance is my number.

Yrs

O. C. Wright.

(Major)

On His Majesty's Service.

OFFICIAL PAID

2nd Lt David Winder Small

Signal Depot

R.E. 24th Div

A.P.O. S1.

Sig. Co.

106 Bde RFA

B.E.F.

If undelivered return to Registration Officer at his address as shown hereon.

Absent voters (including officers but not men in the Forces who have not appointed proxies) should at once notify any change of postal address to the Registration Officer.

Constituency of Hendon (Golders Green)

Polling District Letter

Qualifying Address 57 Golders Green Rd Hendon

FIELD POST OFFICE

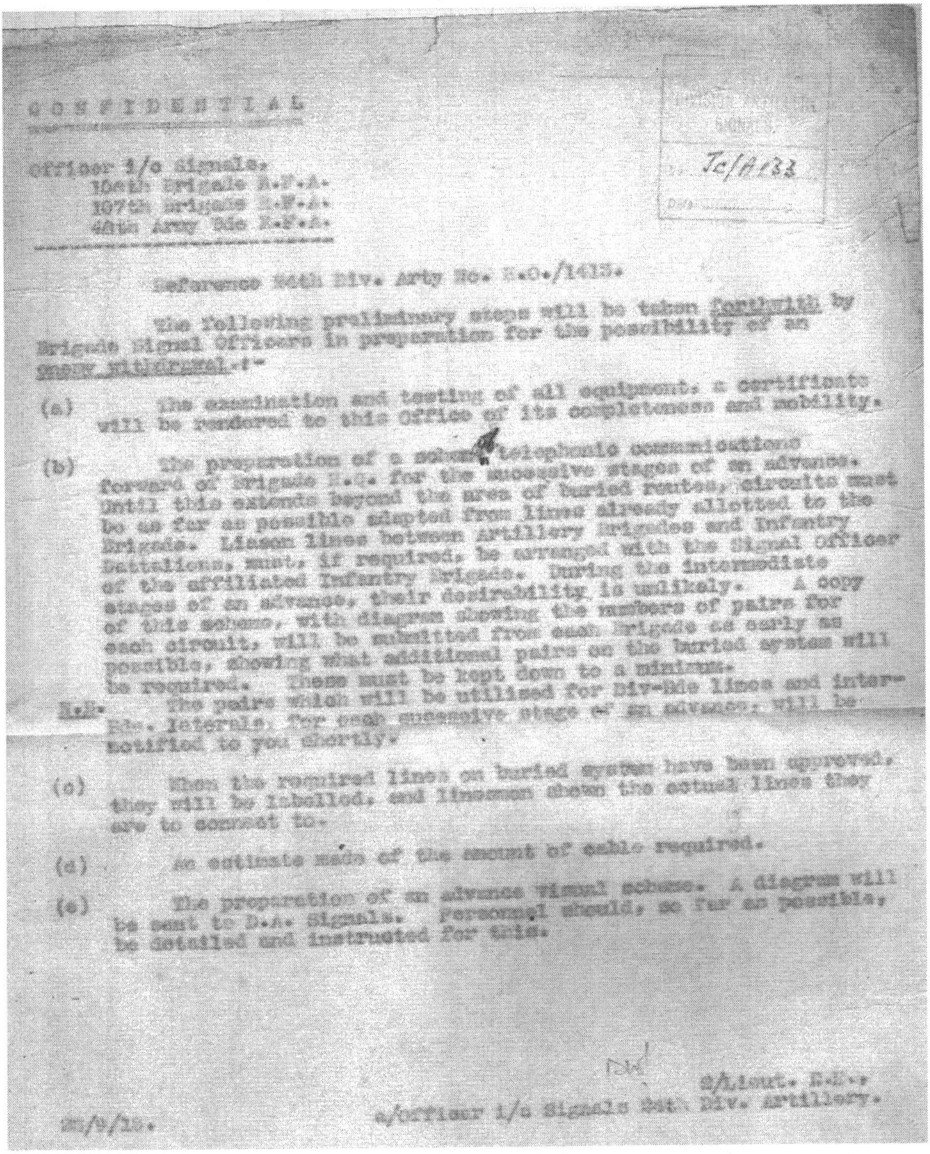

C O N F I D E N T I A L

Officer i/c Signals,
106th Brigade R.F.A.
107th Brigade R.F.A.
48th Army Bde R.F.A.

Jc/A133

Reference 34th Div. Arty No. S.O./1413.

The following preliminary steps will be taken forthwith by Brigade Signal Officers in preparation for the possibility of an enemy withdrawal.:-

(a) The examination and testing of all equipment. A certificate will be rendered to this Office of its completeness and mobility.

(b) The preparation of a scheme telephonic communications forward of Brigade H.Q. for the successive stages of an advance. Until this extends beyond the area of buried routes, circuits must be as far as possible adapted from lines already allotted to the Brigade. Liason lines between Artillery Brigades and Infantry Battalions, must, if required, be arranged with the Signal Officer of the affiliated Infantry Brigade. During the intermediate stages of an advance, their desirability is unlikely. A copy of this scheme, with diagram showing the numbers of pairs for each circuit, will be submitted from each Brigade as early as possible, showing what additional pairs on the buried system will be required. These must be kept down to a minimum.

N.B. The pairs which will be utilised for Div-Bde lines and inter-Bde. laterals, for each successive stage of an advance, will be notified to you shortly.

(c) When the required lines on buried system have been approved, they will be labelled, and linesmen shown the actual lines they are to connect to.

(d) An estimate made of the amount of cable required.

(e) The preparation of an advance visual scheme. A diagram will be sent to D.A. Signals. Personnel should, so far as possible, be detailed and instructed for this.

2/Lieut. R.E.,
a/Officer i/c Signals 34th Div. Artillery.

28/9/18.

Sept: Acting again as OC DA Sigs.

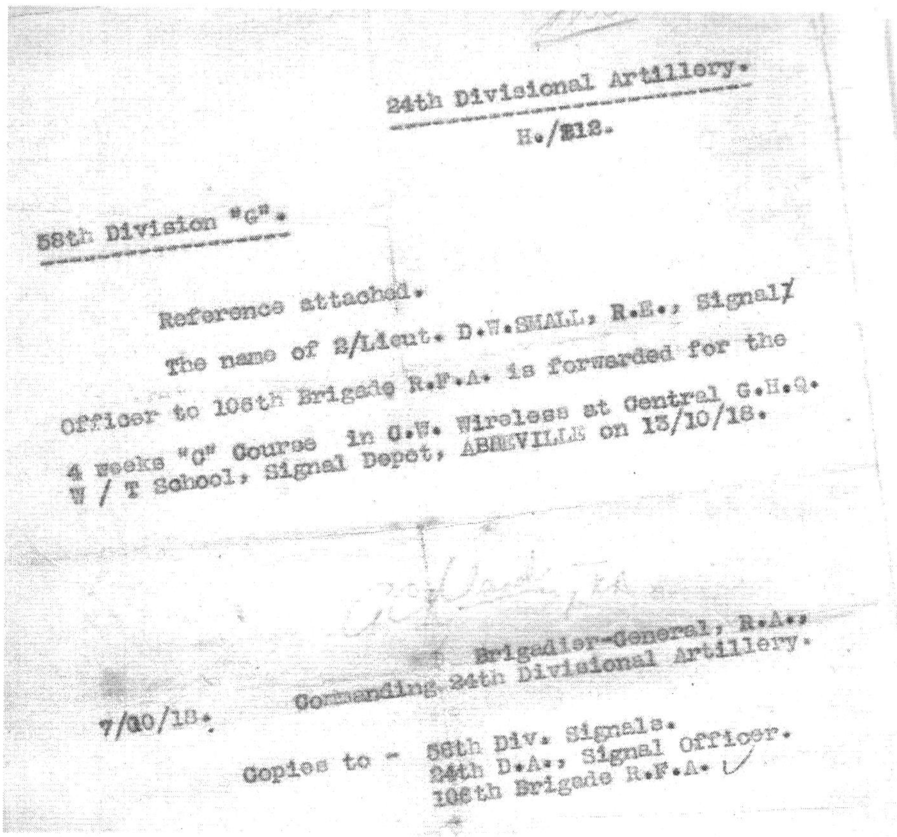
24th Divisional Artillery.

H./E12.

58th Division "G".

Reference attached.

The name of 2/Lieut. D.W.SMALL, R.E., Signal/
Officer to 106th Brigade R.F.A. is forwarded for the
4 weeks "C" Course in C.W. Wireless at Central G.H.Q.
W / T School, Signal Depot, ABBEVILLE on 13/10/18.

Brigadier-General, R.A.,
Commanding 24th Divisional Artillery.

7/10/18.

Copies to - 58th Div. Signals.
24th D.A., Signal Officer.
106th Brigade R.F.A.

Oct: Back at 106 Bde. On Oct 12 went from Bde HQ (then at Hythe Tunnel SE of Loos) to Abbeville for W/T course.

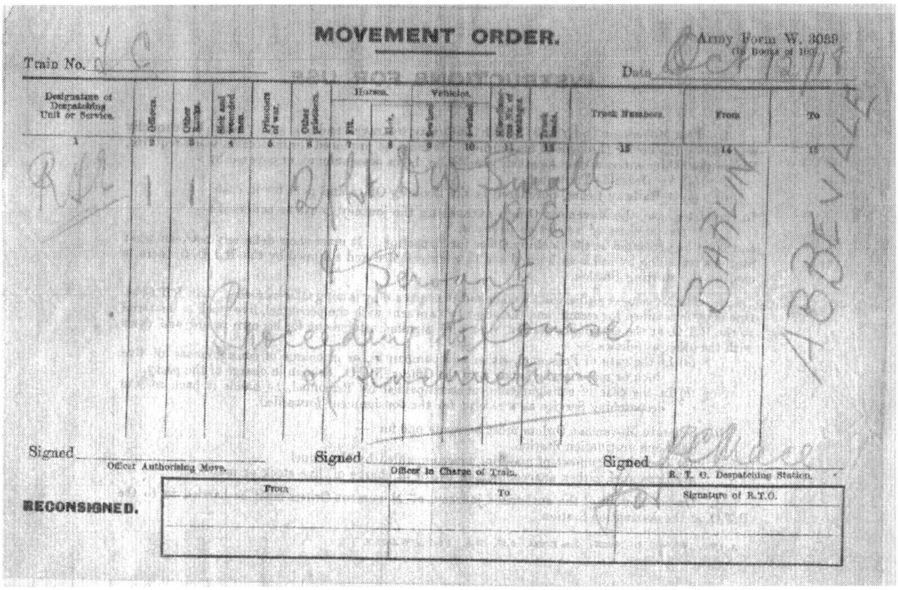

MOVEMENT ORDER.

Army Form W. 3089

Train No.

Date Oct 12/18

BARLIN

ABBEVILLE

Signed ______ Officer Authorising Move.

Signed ______ Officer in Charge of Train.

Signed ______ R. T. O. Despatching Station.

RECONSIGNED.

From	To	Signature of R.T.O.

Nov: Developed blood poisoning at Abbeville and went into hospital, eventually reaching England a few days before the Armistice. (Birkdale Auxiliary Officers Hospital, Southport).

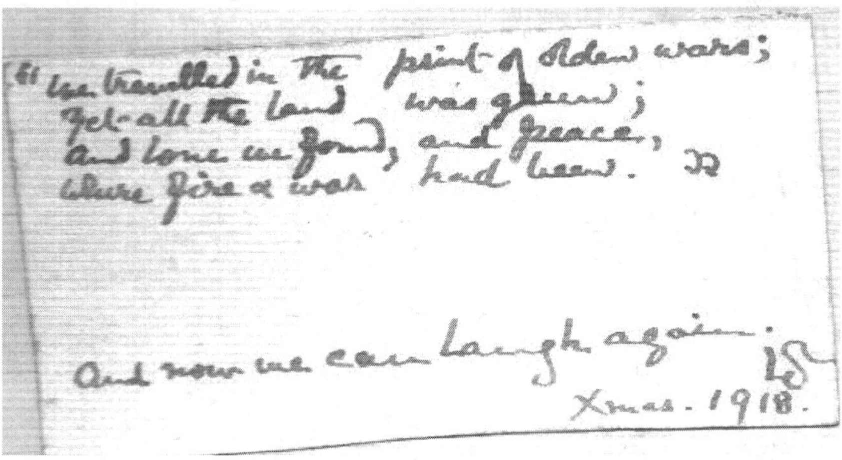

"We travelled in the print of olden wars;
Yet all the land was green;
And love we found, and peace,
Where fire & war had been."

And now we can laugh again.

Xmas. 1918.

Jan 13 1919: Move from Southport to Blake Hall Officers Convalescent Hospital at Ongar.

Blake Hall Officer's Convalescent Hospital 1919

Mar 29: Discharged from hospital.

Apr 23: Demobilised.

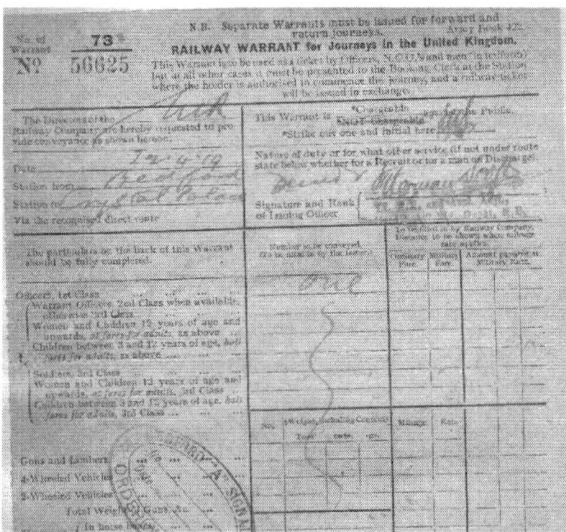

N.B. Separate Warrants must be issued for forward and return journeys.

No. of Warrant 73

Nº 56625

RAILWAY WARRANT for Journeys in the United Kingdom.

The Directors of the Railway Company are hereby requested to provide conveyance as shown hereon.

Date

Station from

Station to

Via the recognised direct route

This Warrant is *Chargeable against the Public. *Strike out one and initial here

Nature of duty or for what other service (if not under route state below whether for a Recruit or for a man on Discharge).

Signature and Rank of Issuing Officer

The particulars on the back of this Warrant should be fully completed.

Officers, 1st Class

Warrant Officers, 2nd Class when available.

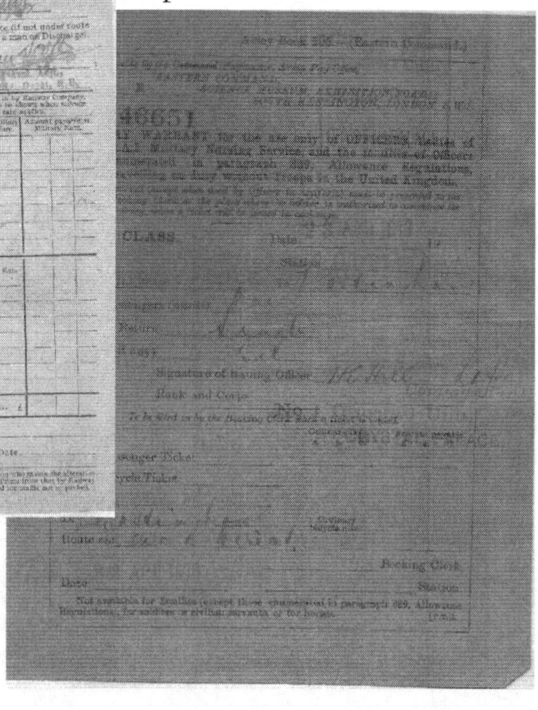

20TH (LIGHT) DIVISION
SIGNAL COMPANY, R.E
18TH ANNUAL RE-UNION.
30TH APRIL 1938.
BROAD ST. STATION RESTAURANT.
LONDON E.C.
MENU.
Soup. Ox Tail
Fish. Fillet of Sole Boitelle
Entree Lamb Cutlets. New Potatoes Spring Greens.
Poultry Roast Chicken & Ham Game Chips.
Sweets. Fruit Salad & Ice Cream
Coffee.
THE KING.
ROYAL ENGINEERS
1916
'17
ESTAMINETS
T.S.R.

LETTERS

Jan 4th 1918

My dear child,

I hope you got back all right. When I returned I found that on Dec 28th poor little Mathews had blown out his brains in his billet. He had orders to return to his battalion on 29th as he hadn't done too well here. He only got back off leave on morning of 28th, and it may have been trouble at home and the order to return to his battalion (which he loathed) was the climax. Anyhow it has upset all of us horribly, more especially myself, as I am one of these very highly strung blokes.

Jumbo was simply splendid and did all that was necessary. RJ has DSO, Baker & Russell DCMs and you probably saw my Brevet? S. your old company (and future one) are fairly cheery, but this tragic business has spoilt things a bit. You were a great success with sis-in-law and brother, I am so glad you came down (or up?). Old d'Andria is going to write to you soon and sends luv. We are still here but not for long, I want to get away and my nerves will be better. Cheers old dear. Write when you have time.

Yours ever,

FR *Cobb.*

15th Nov 1918

My dear Small,

Your letters to Stewart and the Colonel arrived last night. I was very surprised to see by the postmark that you were in England. By refusing to repeat yourself in the letter to Stewart we do not know what is the matter with your poor self. The Colonel has gone on leave and we are therefore in the dark. However I am very sorry to hear that you are queer and trust you will soon be about again.

It is a very long tale to tell you if I detail the whole of our doings since this stunt started, but it has been a very great experience to me – you will be sorry to hear that Davidson, Gudgeon, Hood and Town were all wounded. The first three by a shell which came through the Signal Office in a sunken road near Sepmeries. It was awfully rotten luck. Corporal Hamilton, Harris and Mackenzie are those which have left on account of PUO [pyroxia of unknown origin, medical term usually applied to trench fever]. Corporal Hamilton and Uings both have done splendidly and I am putting their names in for something or other. I hope it will at least be a medal for each.

From the above list you can imagine the work those who were left have had to do especially as Leaphard, Anderson, Richards, Wharmsly and Waldron are away on leave (except Richards). I am writing for Richards at the school today. Sergeant Welch for 4 or 5 days was very queer and I left him at wagon lines.

There are no officers' leaves for the second half of November but I am for one early in December and shall make a point of coming to see you if you will advise any change in your address to my home address:

Stafford House, 26 Cazenove Road, Stamford Hill, London N16. I shall have a lot to tell you and will be very pleased to see you again.

My job now is to supply lists of deficiencies to D/A, together with certificates etc, some job. Stewart will be writing to you today.

Must now close trusting you will soon be fit again and hoping you will write sometime.

Yours, W Lawrence.

PS Wilmott says he's sorry to hear you have finished up over there.

PPS We are moving back tomorrow and so shall take your Kit along with us, should we reach a railhead and then it shall be sent off as you require.

(From Lawrence 2nd Lt RFA of D Bty 106 Bde, who took over the Sig Section when I went into hospital.

Kinglsey Cottage, Eversley, Hants

24/11/18

Dear Small,

Your letter has just been sent on to me and I'm awfully sorry to hear of your bad luck. It is a most unfortunate way to end up the war but I hope you will soon be quite all right again. I suppose it will hardly be worth while you going out again. But if you do, have a try to get back to us. We will give you a great welcome.

I don't know what is going to happen to us now or what the Division is doing as I came off on leave as soon as I could after hostilities ceased and go back again on 28th.

We had a most interesting time for the last 3 or 4 weeks and I'm sorry you had to miss it. Hoping you will soon be well again.

Yours sincerely, JC Walsh.

(From Lt Col Walsh Commanding 106 Bde, RFA)

24/11/18

My dear Small,

Awfully sorry to hear that you are in hospital, though Southport is a nice place, five girls to one man and it should be more now. I was there one Easter and had a ripping time! Heard from Ryan the other day and I believe Cobb is in England.

I don't suppose you will be coming out again as the Boche seems to be about fixed. At any rate my home address is 4 Selborne Grove, Bradford. Tel 1104 Bradford so if it comes about like, that thas'bain near us afta' war's been settled tha'nos and I'm at home gie us a look up, show thee some reet Yorkshire folks an'all.

Still near the coast and leading a very quiet life, wish you were here. Write soon old man!

Yours sincerely, AW d'Andria

PS Your letter was rather delayed, only received it just recently.

From d'Andria, 12th Div Sig Co

Antoing.

January 13 1919

Dear Sir,

I was delighted to receive news of you and thank you very much on behalf of the section for your generous gift of cigarettes; we have no cigarettes in our canteen and no ration cigs yesterday, so you may well imagine how much yours were appreciated.

I paraded the section and read your letter to them and I received a great many suggestions with regard to a suitable reply to you, many of which would, no doubt, make you smile, but of course I am using my own discretion about them and tell you simply that you have their real thanks and appreciation. I learnt some time about Armistice Day of your bad arm and naturally enough expected you to get away with it and when I told the remnants of the section the news, they moaned and groaned considerably for you were very popular.

After leaving Maroc we marched to Cambrai, a three day march with Madame Greenfields as hostess each night; we stayed two or three nights in the Cavalry Barracks at Cambrai, during which time we were receiving very comforting information such as instructions with regard to open warfare and after our comfortable quarters at Maroc we found the going very difficult. Our first position was a village of the name of St Aubert, a few kilometres NE of Cambrai, here nothing happened in particular as far as the section was concerned except HQ got its share of 4.2s and 5.9s from the Boche.

The next position was an advance of about 6 kilometres. I went on in advance and laid wires to batteries, while Cpl Hamilton dismantled the old show and pulled in as much wire as possible. In this position we had rather a bad time of it, the HQ were in the village of Haussy while the batteries were in action just in front of the village. Uings, Town and Davidson accompanied me with the cable cart and we laid one wire from the farthest battery position to HQ's. We had finished our job, the drivers dismounted, I was putting the wire inside the cellar, when a dirty 5.9 came and burst within a few yards, the horses bolted, one hit in the leg and Uings hanging on to their heads like grim death; he eventually guided them into a brick wall and managed to stop them, for which act he has been awarded the Military Medal. We all remember the village of Haussy, it was indeed one of the warmest corners I have been in; Town was gassed and I have heard no further news of him, I fear the worst has happened to him.

Well we managed to push the Boche out of his positions here and made a further advance of about 8 kilometres, which brought us a few kilometres south of Valenciennes. DA at the time were doing rather a funny stunt during these times, more like an advanced Brigade HQ. About Oct 31st we relieved DA of their position and I caught the PUO; we arrived at their place about six o'clock in the evening and I was practically helpless. We had not been in the place more than a quarter of an hour when over came one of those 4.2s and wounded Gudgeon in the hand, Hood in the upper part of the leg and Davidson got several pieces between the knee and the ankle. I have heard from both Davidson and Gudgeon but so far no news from Hood, but I think he is all right, the two former are doing well, Gudgeon is near his home and Davidson in a hospital in France. On the next morning Mr Lawrence sent me down to the wagon line, PUO got me down properly; the same day Anderson went on leave, the next day Waldron, the next Leaphard, imagine then the section: I had received one reinforcement, the usual sort, Wharmsly was already on leave – 4 on leave, 3 wounded and myself hors de combat, but this is not all, Mackenzie got the PUO and went to hospital. I had about 4 days at the wagon line then rejoined again, but did not feel fit for business, so Cpl Hamilton got the brunt of the work. About three days before Armistice Cpl Hamilton got the PUO and he was sent to hospital, I was still unfit so Uings had to carry on. Why I was not sent away I do not know for I could not work for part of the time and this lasted until some few days after Armistice Day. Cpl Hamilton rejoined about a week ago and Mackenzie rejoined two days before Xmas. Cpl Hamilton has the Military Medal also. Warren stuck it all through. Grainger and Dobson and the 3 drivers are also with me. It is a very funny section that we have now, I am glad we have not to go in action with all these reinforcements, I should lose all my hair I am sure.

Uings and Mackenzie are both on leave and personally I do not expect to see them back again and I have a letter of congratulation from the General to Uings. We are doing nothing but playing football now. Everybody wants his ticket and thinks he should be demobilised first. My leave is now about due and I hope to be in England within a week. My officer now is 2nd Lt Gardner, who came from the Machine Gun Corps.

We are all of us in civilian billets. I am quite at home at my place, especially as there are two nice young ladies here, who are always so much concerned in my welfare. We have a fine football team here, a brigade team, we wiped up the Notts & Derby a few days ago, two to nil, a team which has never been beaten before and the section has three men in this team, Anderson, Quinlan (a reinforcement) and myself so we are well represented.

I hope you will excuse the AB 152 paper but one can buy nothing about here, the Boche must have been very badly off, especially when you hear of people making shirts for themselves out of tablecloths.

Well sir, I hope I have missed nothing out in my letter, as far as I can remember this is all that would interest you, so I will conclude my letter with the best of wishes from myself and the section in general.

I remain, Yours very sincerely,

JC Welch

From my Brigade Signal Sergeant

108 High Street, Aylesbury, Bucks

6.4.20

Dear Mr Small,

A word of two to tell you just a wee bit more about myself. I am at present studying at Aylesbury for a short time, still looking out for a job. I joined the REOC and stated my case to them as pur [sic] your instructions, but have heard nothing from them and I have given up hope now. It seems a difficult problem to obtain a situation now. I have written letters galore to advertisers in the various papers, but have not received one reply and it is most disheartening; I am beginning to think my four years in France for my country was not worth the candle, however I suppose people in my position do get a bit cynical at times. I am pleased to say I am in excellent health at the moment but ennui is not the word for it.

I hope you are in good health and that you had a good time this Easter; I remember it's about two years ago since I won you a gas mask and I wonder if you can remember the same incident.

You had no gas mask on joining the 106th Brigade and intimated me of the fact with a request to win one for you if possible; I won one, much to the disgust of the RSM in charge of ordnance stores; such incidents as these are ever recurring in my mind.

I have not heard from any of the late numbers of the Section recently so I have no addresses to give you.

I think this is all now so will conclude with my best wishes.

Yours very sincerely, J C Welch

FROM THE FAMILY ALBUM

David Winder Small: the after effects of gas attacks were with him for the rest of his life.

Phillip Umfreville Laws, born 11 Jan 1895, killed in action 20 Sept 1917. He was awarded the Military Cross - the citation reads:

"For conspicuous gallantry and devotion to duty as Forward Observation Officer. During the action and the five following days he sent in most valuable information as to the enemy's movements, whereby several counter attacks were broken before they could deploy. When the Forward Station Signalling Officer was wounded he also took charge of the signals and kept up communication with the brigade, remaining at his post after the troops on his right had been forced to fall back. By his coolness, able leadership and excellent reports he was largely instrumental in making the flank secure and clearing up the situation". Near Ypres 31st July 1917

Summer 1921 David and Olivia Laws are newly engaged and involved in amateur theatricals with other members of the family under the leadership of Sandy and Dorothy Henniker - the local Squire and his wife - who were their nearest neighbours. Rehearsals were usually at the Hall but a big tithe barn made quite a usable theatre. David & Olivia married on 31st July 1922.

Cast of "His Excellency" Left to Right Back Row: Geoffrey Laws, Jack Heath, Olivia Laws, John Laws [my father], David Small, Captain Wilson; Front Row: Mr Falcon, Dorothy Kentish Wright, Sandy Henniker, Dorothy Henniker.

Evan William Small,
David's father

David, Geoffrey Laws, Jim Foley & Olivia circa 1928; Geoffrey & Jim on leave from the tinfields of the Bauchi Plateau in Nigeria.

Olivia outside their first marital home, a basement flat at 38a Warrington Crescent, London, W9. Here their only child Roger was born on 27th October 1923. It was quite a nice flat with a patch of garden at the back, a priceless asset in W9 even then. All day and far into the night deep rumbles came from the earth where the Northern Line must have passed almost directly below.

David's mother Maria Louise Small (née Winder) outside the house in Mill Hill to which she moved when widowed.

David & Olivia outside their cottage at Bovingdon to which they moved soon after Roger was born.

Roger
1937

David and Roger circa 1938

CLOSE FAMILY TREE

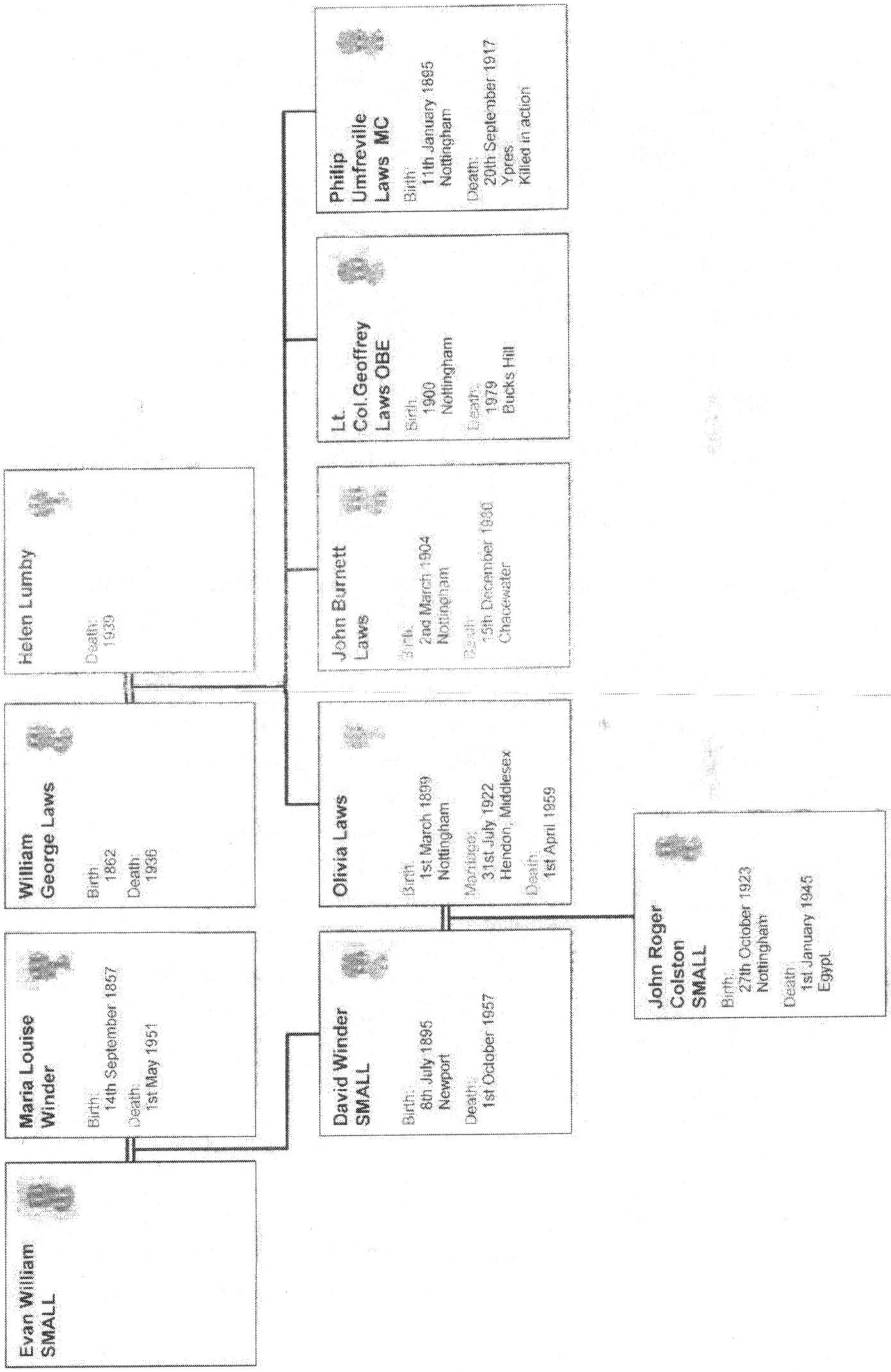

OFFICIAL PAPERS

David's Birth & War Service Certificates

57441

CERTIFIED COPY of an ENTRY OF BIRTH.
Pursuant to the Births and Deaths Registration Acts, 1836 to 1874.

Registration District NEWPORT, MON.

1895. Birth in the Sub-District of Newport in the County of Monmouth

No.	When and Where Born.	Name, if any.	Sex.	Name and Surname of Father.	Name and Maiden Surname of Mother.	Rank or Profession of Father.	Signature, Description and Residence of Informant.	When Registered.	Signature of Registrar.
2	Eighth July 1895 36 Bassaley Road Newport U.D.	David Winder	Boy	Evan William Small	Maria Louisa Small formerly Winder	Director of Technical Instruction	Evan W. Small Father 36 Bassaley Road Newport	Twentieth July 1895	E.C. Wring Deputy Registrar

I, ARTHUR O. PARRY Superintendent Registrar for the District of NEWPORT in the Counties of MONMOUTH do hereby certify that this is a true copy of the Entry No. 2 in the Register Book of Births No. 117 for the above-named Sub-district, and that such Book is now legally in my custody.

WITNESS MY HAND this 17th day of October 1921

D.W.SMALL. **CERTIFICATE OF WAR SERVICE.** JAN. 1915 – APR. 1919

I certify that D.W.Small was with the 20th Divisional Signal Company R.E. as Instructor of French and German to the 20th Divisional Royal Engineers from JANUARY 20th 1915 to JUNE 20th 1915.

On June 21st 1915 he enlisted in the Royal Engineers and served in the 20th Divisional Signal Company as a Corporal (Regimental Number: 54,444) until July 1916 when he left the unit in France and was invalided to England.

Having undergone a course of Instruction in England as a Cadet, he was gazetted Second Lieutenant on August 1st 1917 and served as an Officer with the 24th Divisional Signal Company and other units until his demobilisation on April 24th 1919.

F. J. M. Stratton
Senior Tutor, Gonville & Caius
College Cambridge

1923, March 29.

formerly Lt-Colonel, Royal Engineers
Chief Signal Officer, XIXth Corps,
B.E.F. France

David & Olivia's Marriage Certificate

B 178366

CERTIFIED COPY of an ENTRY OF MARRIAGE. Pursuant to the Marriage Acts, 1836 to 1898.

Registration District Hendon

1922. Marriage Solemnized at the Register Office in the District of Hendon in the County of Middlesex

No.	When Married.	Name and Surname.	Age.	Condition.	Rank or Profession.	Residence at the time of Marriage.	Father's Name and Surname.	Rank or Profession of Father.
22	Thirty first July 1922	David Windor Small	27 years	Bachelor	Secondary Schoolmaster	9 Alba Gardens Golders Green	Evan William Small	[illegible]
		Olivia Laws	23 years	Spinster	—	9 Alba Gardens Golders Green	William George Laws	[illegible]

Married in the Register Office ~~according to the Rites and Ceremonies of the~~ by licence before me

This Marriage was solemnized between us, David W. Small, O. Laws; in the Presence of us, [illegible], [illegible]; W. R. Hurst Registrar, T. J. Seabrook Superintendent Registrar

I, Wilfred R. Hurst, Registrar of Marriages for the District of Hendon, in the County of Middlesex do hereby certify that this is a true copy of the Entry No. 22 in the Register Book of Marriages for the said District, and that such Register Book is now legally in my custody.

WITNESS MY HAND this 31st day of July, 1922.

W. R. Hurst

Roger's Birth Certificate

GA 515355

CERTIFIED COPY of an ENTRY of BIRTH.

SUPPLIED AT THE SPECIAL FEE OF 6d. APPLICABLE IN CERTAIN STATUTORY CASES.

THIS CERTIFICATE IS ISSUED FOR THE PURPOSES OF Elementary Education and for NO OTHER USE OR PURPOSES WHATEVER.

Registration District NOTTINGHAM.

1923 BIRTH in the Sub-District of NOTTINGHAM. South West in the County of NOTTINGHAM.

No.	When and where born	Name (if any)	Sex	Name and Surname of Father	Name and Maiden Surname of Mother	Rank or Profession of Father	Signature, Description and Residence of Informant	When Registered	Signature of Registrar	Baptismal Name if added after Registration of Birth
399	Twenty-Seventh October 1923 6 Oxford Street U.D.	John Roger Colston	Boy	David Windor Small	Olivia Small formerly Laws	School Master 38a Warrington Crescent London W.9	O. Small Mother 38a Warrington Crescent London W.9	Twenty Seventh November 1923	J. O. Saxby Registrar.	

I hereby certify that the above is a true Copy of an Entry of Birth in a Register Book in my custody.

Witness my hand this 17th day of September 1934

Superintendent

CAUTION.—Any person who (1) falsifies any of the particulars on this Certificate or (2) uses it as true knowing it to be false, is liable to prosecution.

Roger's first passport

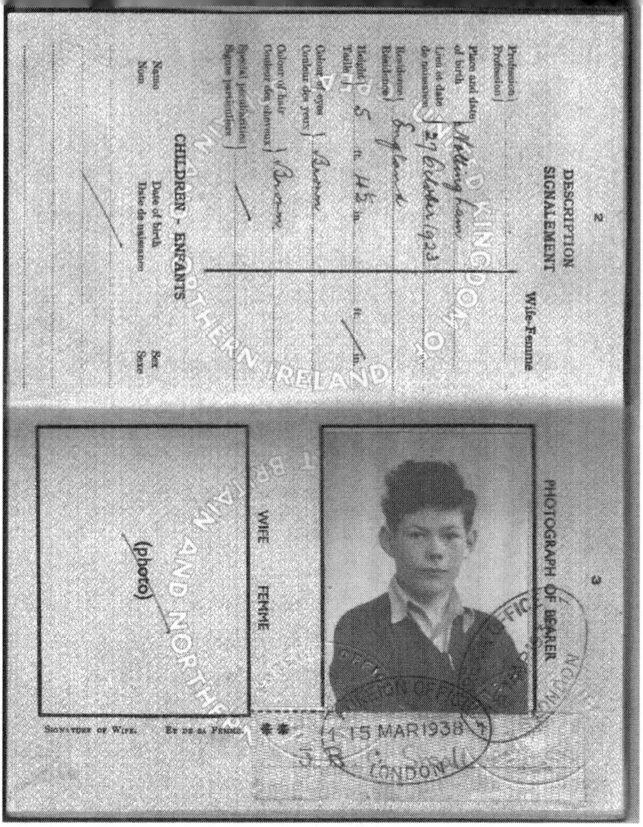

Stunning portrait of Roger [I guess] just before he joined up.

Various Christmas Cards produced at Haberdashers' Aske's

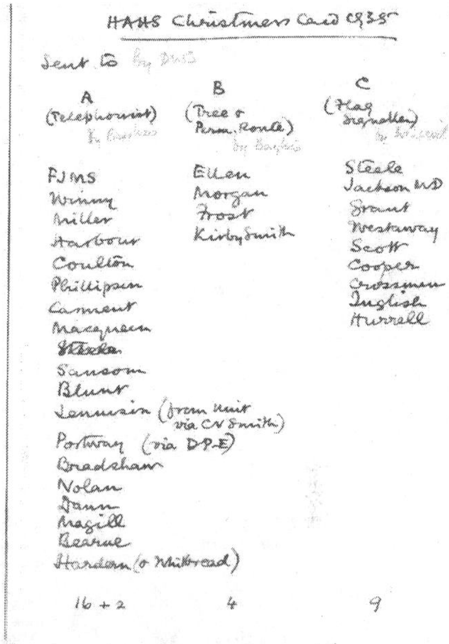

HAHS Christmas Card c1935

Sent to

A (Telephonist)	B (Tree & Perm. Route)	C (Flag Signaller)
FJMS	Ellen	Steele
Winny	Morgan	Jackson WD
Miller	Frost	Grant
Harbour	Kirby Smith	Westaway
Coulton		Scott
Phillipson		Cooper
Cament		Crossman
Macqueen		English
~~Steele~~		Hurrell
Sansom		
Blunt		
Lennuin (from unit via CV Smith)		
Portway (via DP-E)		
Bradshaw		
Nolan		
Dann		
Magill		
Bearne		
Hardam (& Whitbread)		
16 + 2	4	9

CHRISTMAS GREETINGS 1936

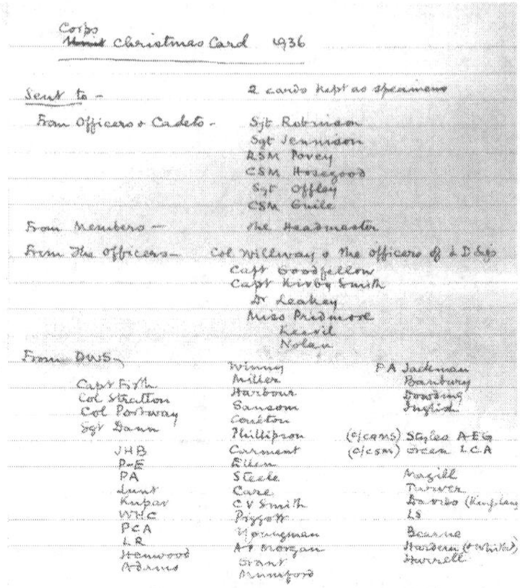

~~Unit~~ Corps Christmas Card 1936

Sent to – 2 cards kept as specimens

From Officers & Cadets – Sgt Robinson
Sgt Jennison
RSM Povey
CSM Hazegood
Sgt Offley
CSM Guile

From Members – the Headmaster

From the Officers – Col Willway & the officers of 4 D Gds
Capt Goodfellow
Capt Kirby Smith
Dr Leakey
Miss Pridmore
Keavil
Nolan

From DWS –
Capt Firth
Col Stratton
Col Portway
Sgt Dann
JHB
P-E
PA
Lunt
Kupar
WHC
PCA
LR
Henwood
Adams

Winney
Miller
Harbour
Sansom
Coulton
Phillipson
Carment
Ellen
Steele
Case
CV Smith
Piggott
Youngman
AT Morgan
Grant
Munford

PA Jackman
Banbury
Dowding
English
(c/cqms) Styles AEG
(c/csm) Green LCA
Magill
Turner
Davies (Kingsley
LS
Bourne
Harden (& White)
Harrell

CHRISTMAS GREETINGS

CHRISTMAS GREETINGS

CHRISTMAS GREETINGS

Third from left, David the old soldier back in uniform as a Captain in the Home Guard.

David on night operation with the Home Guard in 1943.

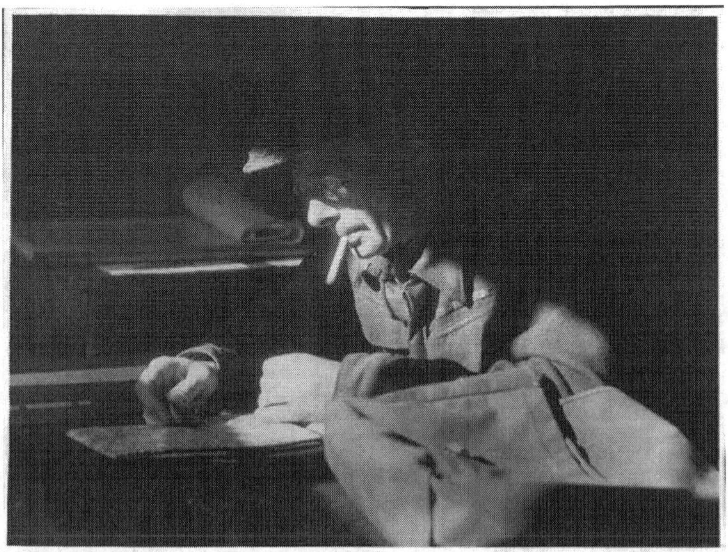

Probably immediately post war - for David and Olivia the war had taken their only son, Roger killed in a crash on an Egyptian airfield whilst training to be a pilot in the RAF in January 1945.

Roger's medals

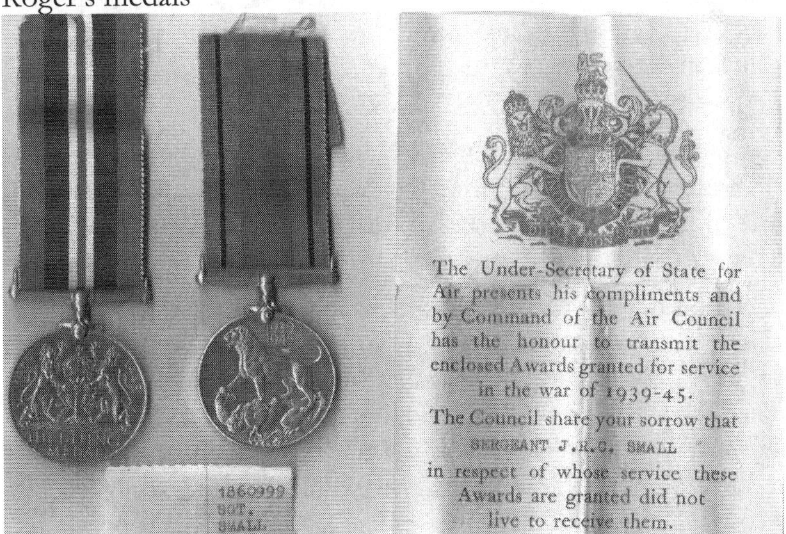

NOTEBOOKS

Extracts from DAS's memos etc (from working note book) –

Buried systems: one mains route per Div front, 6´ deep, less than that gives endless trouble.

In shelled areas overland ladder lines often hold. Good plan to lay 3 parallel lines 15 yds apart and ladder with lines every 50 yds. Must patrol every part of ladder twice daily and mend all breaks.

Visual: Have stations transmitting to a flank to obviate DD [double density] messages. Generally waste of men to provide long chain of stations between Bde and Div.

Power Buzzer: good if confidence placed in it. Burying bases often advantageous. Accumulators.

Forward Comms: SS148 followed in main by establishment of Bde Forward Stn, one on front of each attacking Bde. Subject to alterations in details however. As a rule cables not laid out immediately behind attacking troops as this resulted in cables being badly cut by hostile barrage. Also inadvisable to send PB and Amplifier forward at Zero as party nearly always broken up by shell fire, and if one member fails to arrive set is useless. Best scheme is to keep telephone and PB-Amp parties under the farthest forward available cover until about Zero + 1 hour, ie until first objective has been reached. They can then move forward selecting the thin places in the barrage and establish themselves prior to attack on succeeding objectives.

Very desirable to attach permanently signallers from battns to Bde Sectn in order that the latter may be always ready to take on any work that it may be called on to perform, without having to call on men whose capabilities are unknown.

DAS 199 Telegrams to Police Authorities. GRO 2145 20/2/17. If necessary to telegraph to police in England requiring an answer by wire, insert RP (reply paid) followed by number of words authorised for reply, before address, eg. RP10 Chief Constable Manchester. This only for urgent cases. If police confirmation required for application for special leave, RP telegram should be sent through French PO at expense of individual concerned. Has been arranged that answers from police to RP telegrams through

French PO will be forwarded over military wires instead of by post at base.

DAS circulated memo 140 6/9/16

Cable GP No 14 concentric MkI 1. copper conductor 14 SWG, 2. GP insulation, 3. copper tape, 4. tarred tape, 5. piano wire armouring.

Insulation between 3 and 4 being very low, circuits in which 3 is used as a return must be treated as earth return circuits as regards overhearing by amplifiers.

A new type (Mk II) differs in having GP instead of tarred tape for 4. Central conductor and copper strip therefore form a true insulated metallic circuit.

GHQ letter OB/618 10/11/15

O i/c Sigs with each formation down to Infy Bdes acts as Staff Officer for all questions affecting Signal communication to the GOC formation. His duties include co-ordination and supervision of signal work not only of signal service but of all Arty, Infy and other units under command of his GOC.

Duties of Signalmaster i/c Bde Signal Office:

1. Responsible for general conduct of office and proper disposal of all messages and DRLS. Read all telegrams and note any changes of address.
2. Inform Bde Office whenever post or DRLS about to start.
3. Inform NCO i/c Lines of any dis at once.
4. Report difficulty in getting messages through and notify senders early of any delay or failure to dispose of messages.
5. When working to or in danger zone will be responsible that messages contain no names of units or information useful to the enemy.
6. Show copies of all telegrams relating to operations, movement of units, or containing other important information, to Sig Offr as soon as possible.
7. Consult a Sig Offr when in doubt, report to him any line dis or other occurrence affecting work of office, deliver to him all possible urgent matter which arrives during night.
8. Keep roster of orderlies and operators.
9. Operate phone exchange.
10. Stop all unnecessary talking.

Red Line.* Route taken by the 20th Div. when Div. on move. Sig Coy. R.E.

Blue Line. Roads traversed carrying Despatches & otherwise.

● Divisional Headquarters.

✚ Brigade Headquarters at which D.W.S. was stationed.

Billets. Names underlined with red.

* Larkhill - Southampton - Havre (July 20 1915)
Havre - Lumbres (train, July 21-22)
Lumbres - Lynde - Merris (Aug. '15)
Merris - Nouveau Monde (Estaires) (Sept. Oct. '15)
N^eau Monde - Sailly-sur-Lys (Nov. Dec. '15)
Sailly - Blaringhem (divisional rest) (Jan '16)
Blaringhem - Oxelaere (Jan '16)
Oxelaere - Esquelbecq (Jan '16)
Esquelbecq - Poperinghe-Elverdinghe road (Feb. Mar. Apr.)
Elv. road - Esquelbecq (divisional rest) May '16
Esquelbecq - Poperinghe (June, July '16).

Division contains 12 to 14000 men.

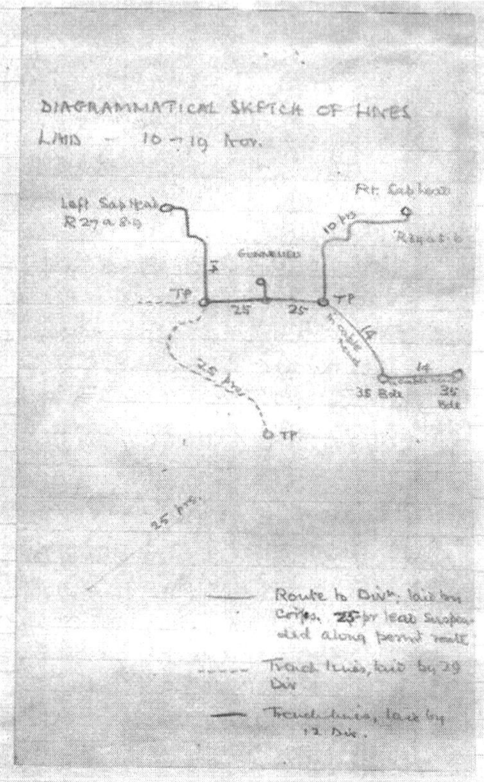

Page from original diary from which letterpress of this book on Oct 27 1917 is copied

ALL SERVICES.

Requisition or Issue Voucher for Stores.

Received from } Cadet Small D.W.
Required
by } Discharged to Commission the
for
undermentioned Stores.

No.	Description.
1	Great Coat Warm
1	Boots
2	Jackets S.D.
1	Pantaloons
1	Spurs
1	Kit Bag deficient

24/7/17

for Cpl ... R.E.

Signature ______
Rank ______
Date ______

This portion of the Voucher to be retained by the Officer in charge of Stores.

N.B.—The necessary alteration should be made in the heading of this form according to the service for which it is required.

Mr. D. W. Small,
Royal Engineers.

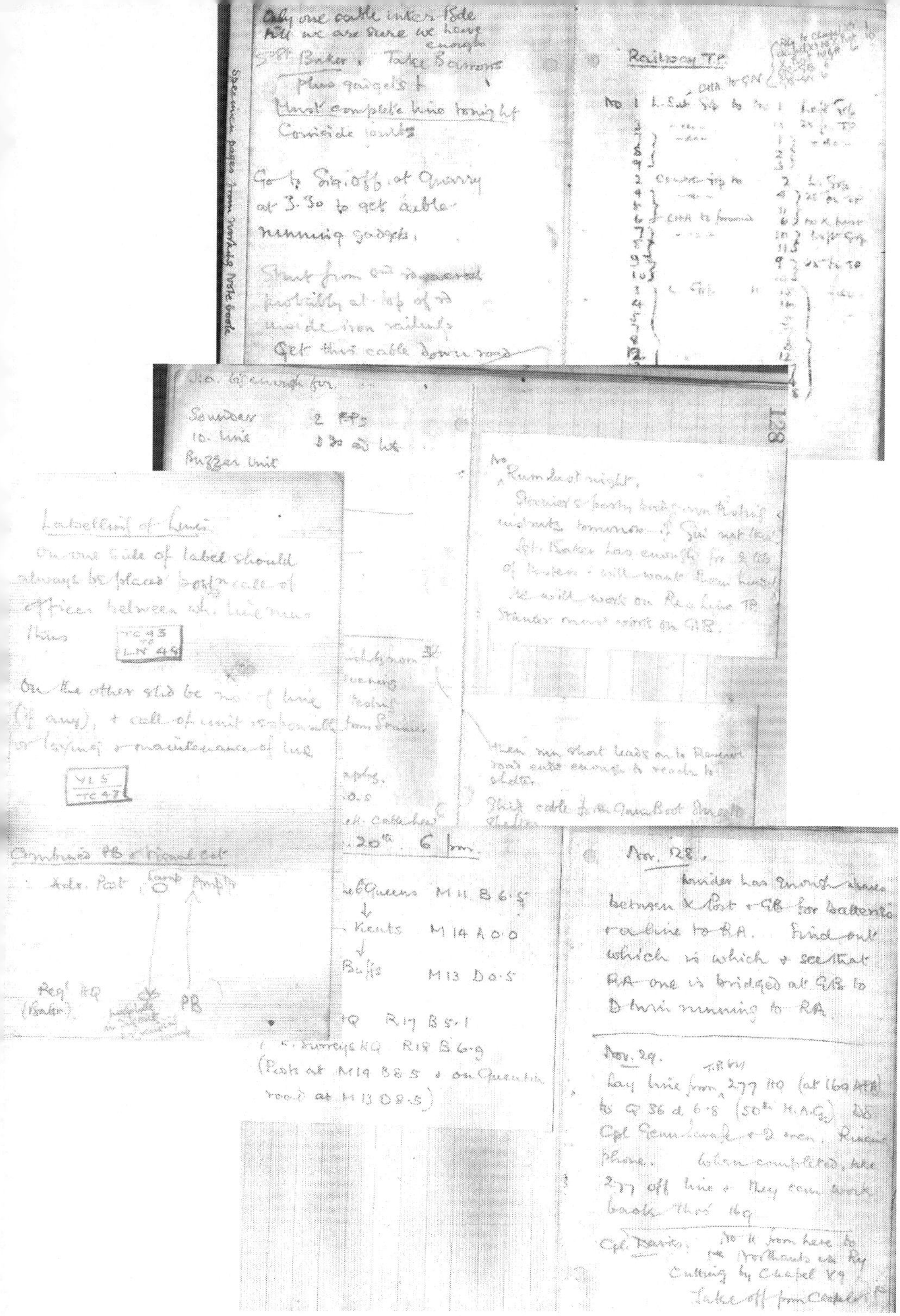
Specimen pages from working note book
Only one cable inter-Bde till we are sure we have enough
Sgt Baker. Take Barrows plus gadgets
Must complete line tonight
Consider joints
Go to Sig. Off. at Quarry at 3.30 to get cable-running gadgets.
Start from our road probably at top of rd inside iron railings
Get this cable down road
Railway T.P.
CHA to GN
Lots of enough for.
Sounder 2 FPs
Buzzer Unit
Labelling of Lines.
On one side of label should always be placed posit. call of offices between wh. line runs thus
TC 43 to LN 49
On the other shd be no. of line (if any), + call of unit responsible for laying + maintenance of line
YL 5 / TC 47
Combined PB + Signal Off
Adv. Post
Lamp
Ampli
Regl HQ (Baker)
PB
No Rum last night.
Then run short leads on to Reserve road enough to reach to shelter.
Thick cable from Gun Boot Store to shelter
20th 6 pm.
Queens M 11 B 6.5
Kents M 14 A 0.0
Buffs M 13 D 0.5
HQ R 17 B 5.1
Surreys HQ R 18 B 6.9
(Posts at M 19 B 8.5 + on Quentin road at M 13 D 8.5)
Nov. 28.
between X Post + GB for batteries + a line to RA. Find out which is which + see that RA one is bridged at GB to D line running to RA.
Nov. 29.
Lay line from T.P. 64 277 HQ (at 169 AFB) to Q 36 d. 6.8 (50th H.A.G.)
Cpl
phone. When completed, take 277 off line + they can work back thro' 169
Cpl. Davis. No 11 from here to 5th Northants in Ry Cutting by Chapel X9.
Take off from Chapel

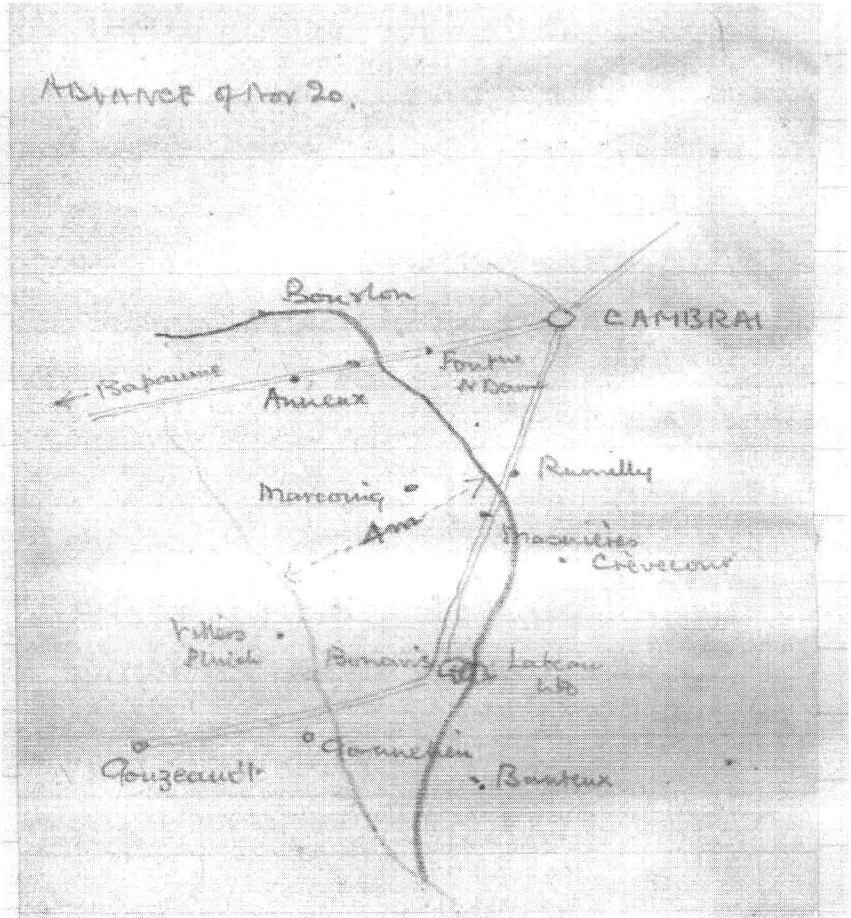
ADVANCE of Nov 20.
Bourlon
CAMBRAI
Bapaume
Anneux
Fontaine N Dame
Rumilly
Marcoing
Masnières
Crèvecour
Villers Pluich
Bonavis
Lateau Wd
Gonnelieu
Gouzeaucourt
Banteux

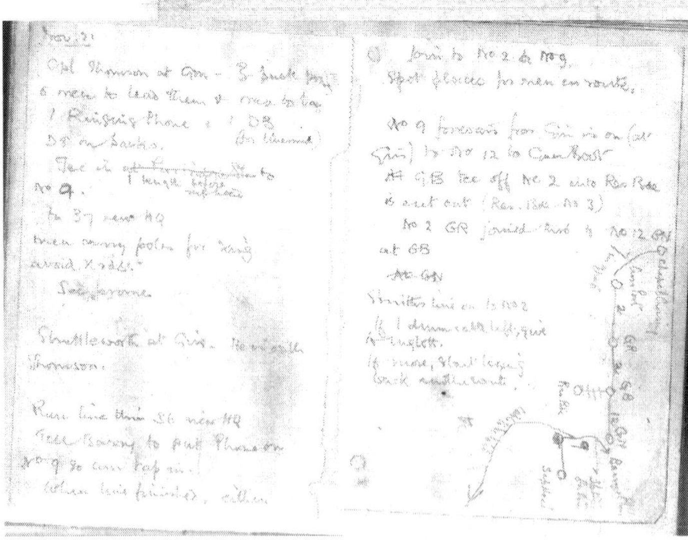

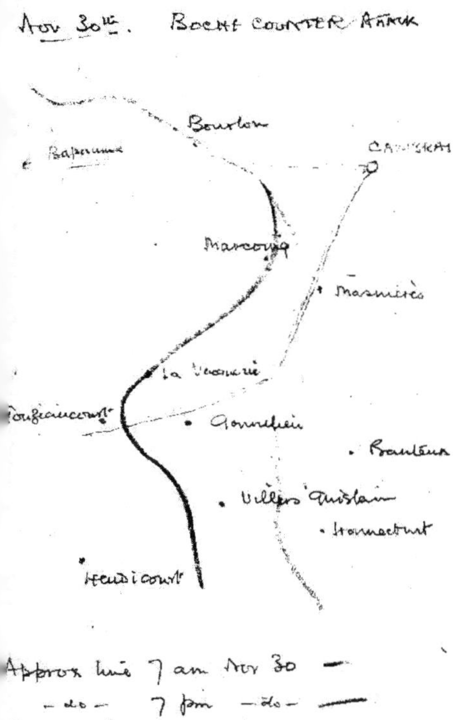

from my original diary.

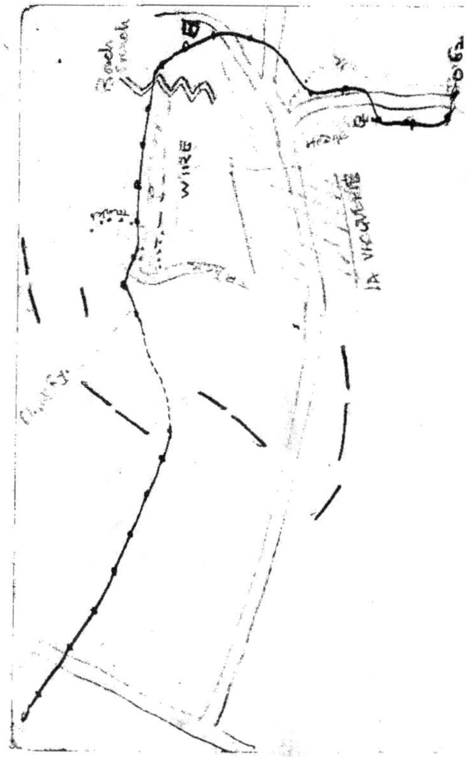

...querie portion of line laid Nov 21. From working note book

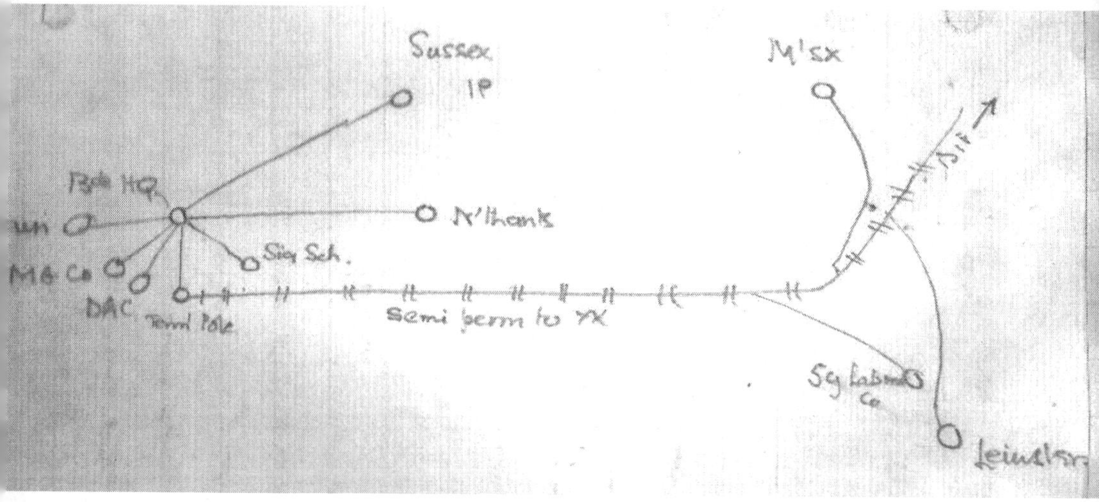

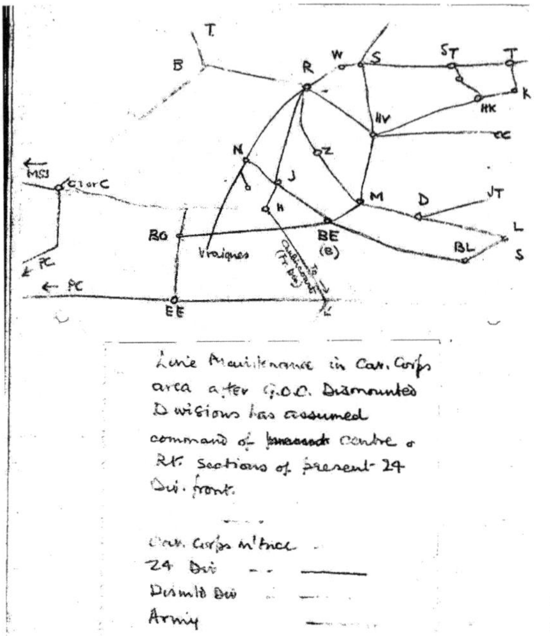

[illegible]

1. [illegible]
2. [illegible] 5 Div
3.
4
5 [illegible] 5 & 6, 10 & 11 fault out 200x GN side of Partridge St
6.
7 [illegible]

[illegible]

9. [illegible]
10 [illegible]
11 [illegible]
12. → spare [illegible] (RFA, exchange)
13 [illegible] to 35 Battery
14. [illegible] Exchange (Foo)

Green Switch T.P.

Right through — 1-6

7 to Position 36
8 Back to No 4 to R. Grp
9 -do- 20 to GN
10 -do- 13 to R. Grp
11 -do- 11 -do-
12 ~~Spare~~ from GS to No 5 FR at [illegible]
13 Back 13 to GN
14 ~~Spare~~ split at GS. 63 Bde forward. Back to [illegible] at [illegible]
15 } Back 15 } to GN
16 16
17 17
18 8
19 9 [illegible]
20 Spare
21 } Back 21 } to GN
22 22
23 23
24 24
25 25
1 } to R. Grp 11 } to GN
2 -do- 12
3 7
5 } -do- 1 } up road to GB
6 2
7 3
8 } -do- 18 } GN
9 19
10 10
14 14

4, 5, 6 by road to GB as spare

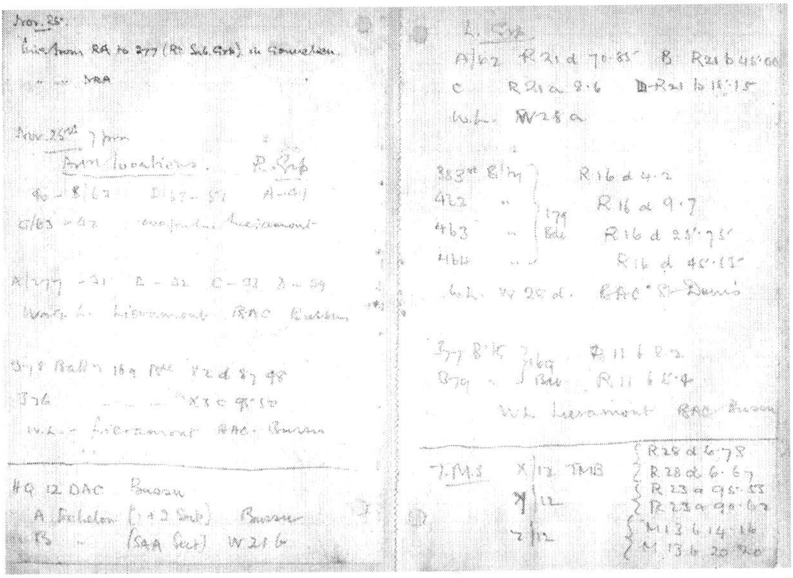

Nov. 25.

Line from RA to 277 (Rt Sub Grp) in Gouzeaucourt

Nov. 25th 7 pm

Bttn locations. R. Grp

G/83 – 42

A/277 – 31 B – 32 C – 33 D – 39

W.L. Lieramont RAC Buscu

378 Battn 169 Bde X2 d 87 98

376 X3 c 95 50

W.L. Lieramont RAC Buscu

HQ 12 DAC Buscu

A Echelon (1 + 2 Sub) Buscu

B – (SAA Sect) W21 b

L. Grp

A/62 R21 d 70·85 B R21 b 45·00

C R21 a 8·6 D R21 b 15·15

W.L. W28 a

383rd B'y R16 d 4·2

422 " } 179 Bde R16 d 9·7

463 " R16 d 25·75

466 " R16 d 45·15

W.L. W25 d. RAC St Denis

377 B'ty } 169 Bde R11 b 8·2

379 " R11 b 5·4

W.L. Lieramont RAC Buscu

T.M.s X/12 TMB { R28 d 6·78, R28 d 6·67 }

Y/12 { R23 a 95·55, R23 a 90·67 }

Z/12 { M13 b 14·16, M13 b 20·20 }

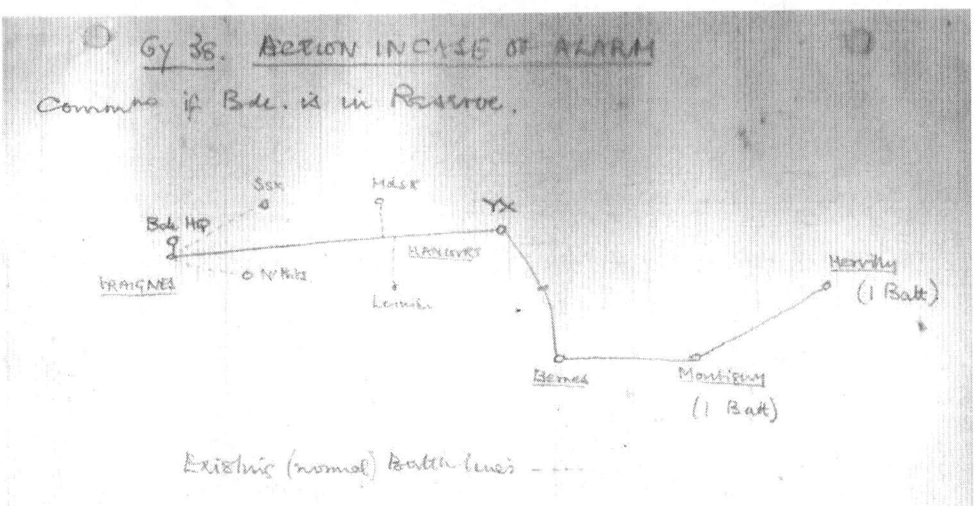

R.A. A.P Detn.

56255 Sgt Marshall G.

357366 L/Cpl. Flood H.C.F.

253657 L/Cpl Richards A.C. ✓

153655 Spr Clark G.

253656 Spr. Wellham C.

253658 Spr Minty T

207278 Spr Collis J.T.

50318 Spr. Hannah J.

50304 Spr. Kirk F.

49752 Spr Little J.H.

75481 Spr. Ridgway A

47041 Spr Smith G.W. ✓

78960 Spr Spencer T.V.

448226 Spr Thomas D.W. ✓

598566 Spr Sadler H.

109008 Gnr Wellham F.

173424 Dvr Cox H

141219 Dvr Nixon J

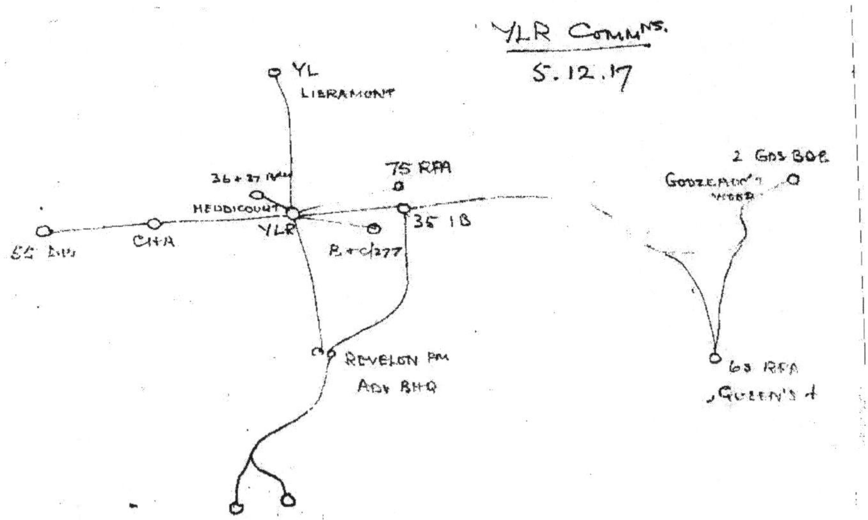
YLR COMMNS.
5.12.17
YL
LIBRAMONT
HEUDICOURT
YLR
75 RFA
35 IB
CHA
REVELON FM
ADV BHQ
2 GDS BDE
63 RFA

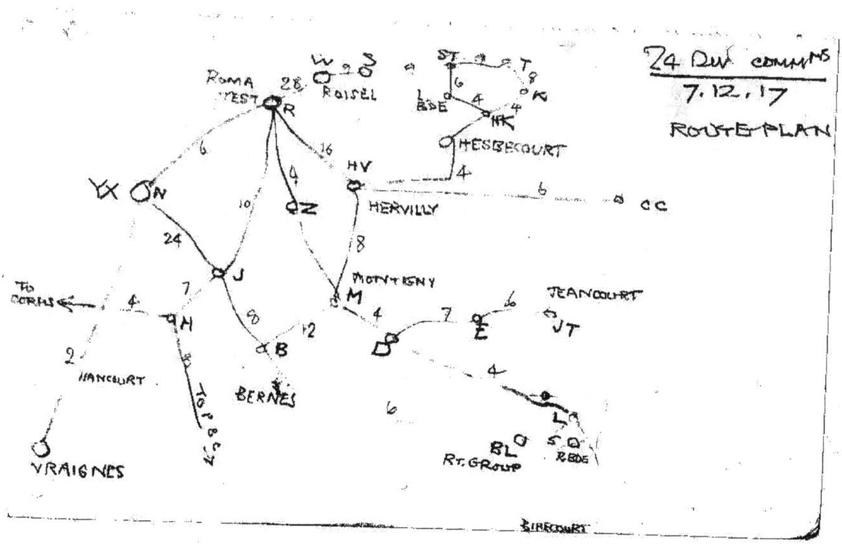
24 DIV COMMNS
7.12.17
ROUTE PLAN
ROMA
R
ROISEL
ST
T
K
HK
HESBECOURT
HV
HERVILLY
CC
YX
N
Z
J
MONTIGNY
M
TO CORPS
H
B
BERNES
D
E
JEANCOURT
JT
HANCOURT
VRAIGNES
L
BL
RT GROUP
BDE

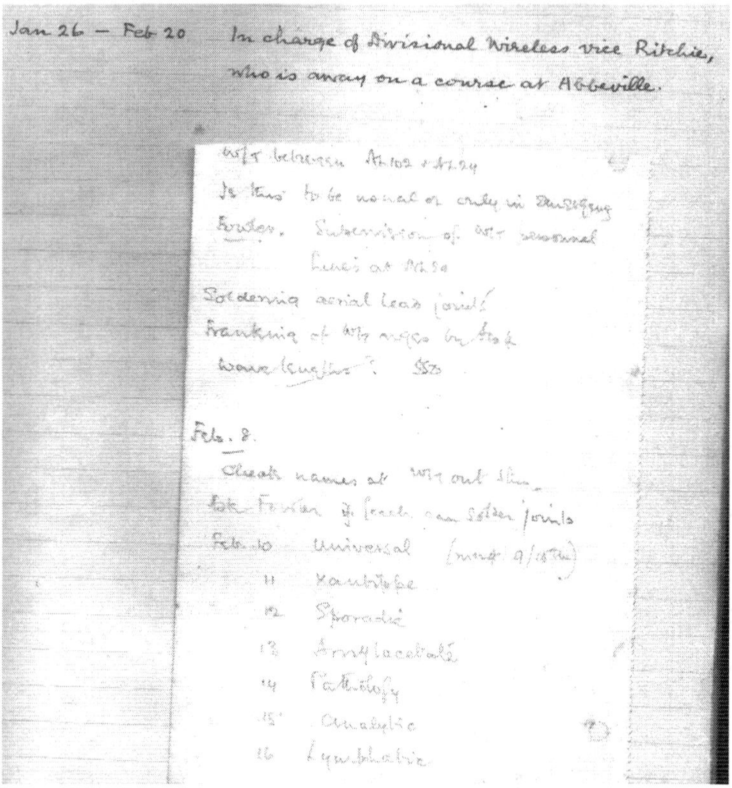

Jan 26 – Feb 20 In charge of Divisional Wireless vice Ritchie, who is away on a course at Abbeville.

W/T between ... 102 & ... 24

Is this to be normal or only in emergency

Orders. Supervision of W/T personnel

Lines at ...

Soldering aerial lead joints

Franking of W/T msgs by ...

Wave lengths? ...

Feb. 8.

Check names at W/T out stns.

... Fowler ... French can solder joints

Feb. 10 Universal (... 9/18th)

11 Xanthippe

12 Sporadic

13 Amylacetate

14 Pathology

15 Analytic

16 Lymphatic

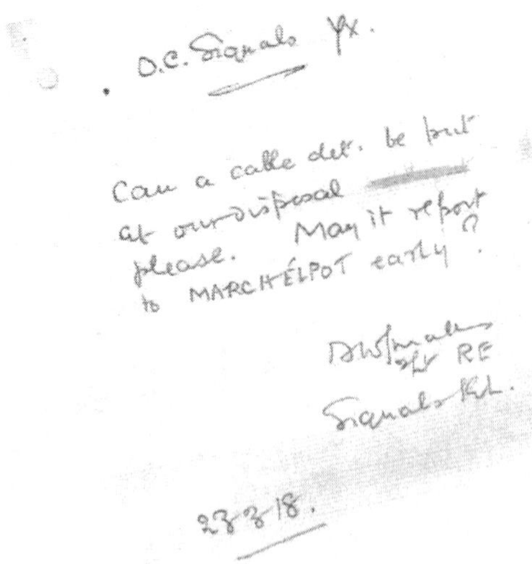

O.C. Signals Yx.

Can a cable det. be put at our disposal please. May it report to MARCHÉLPOT early?

D.W. ...
... RE
Signals ...

2.3.18.

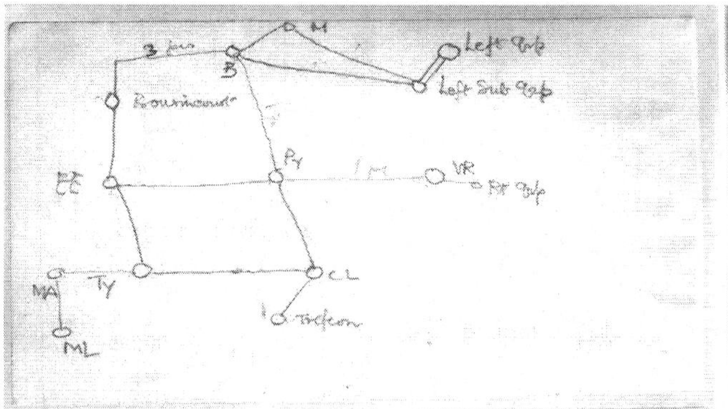

From	To	
KL	Left Gp	VG 7/8 – Bo BE 7/8 – BL 5/4 – Cable to Gp
KL	L. Sub Gp	VG 5/6 – Bo BE 5/6 – BM 1/2 – MD 19/20 – MD BL 11/12
KL	Right Gp	VG 21/22 – Bo BE 9/10 – BE PY – PY VR – VR VD
~~KL~~		~~VG 3/4 – Bo EE 13/14 – EE PY 10/13 – PY VR~~ ?
KL	Wagon lines Trefcon	
KL	DAC	VG 3/4 – Bo EE 13/14 – EE TY 7/8 – TY-CL-TN Cable
QF	Wagon lines [illegible]	Cable to VR – VR PY 12/15 – PY CL 3/4
KL	Rgt Gp (2)	Bo-EE – EE PY 10/13 – PY VR ?

24 DA lines from Bourincourt

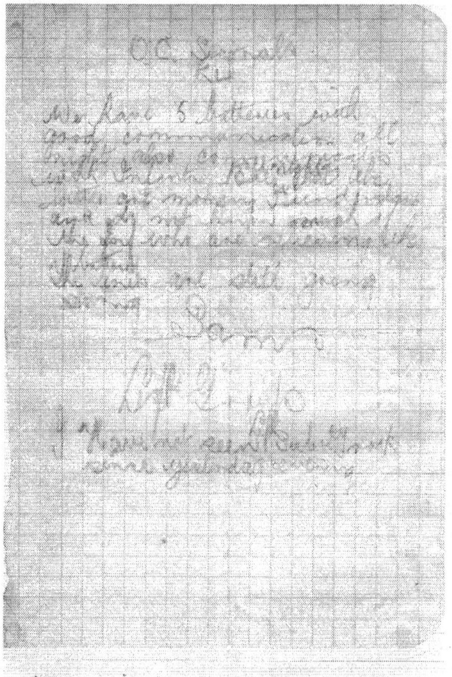

Message received from Sams, Sig Offr 311 Arty Bde.

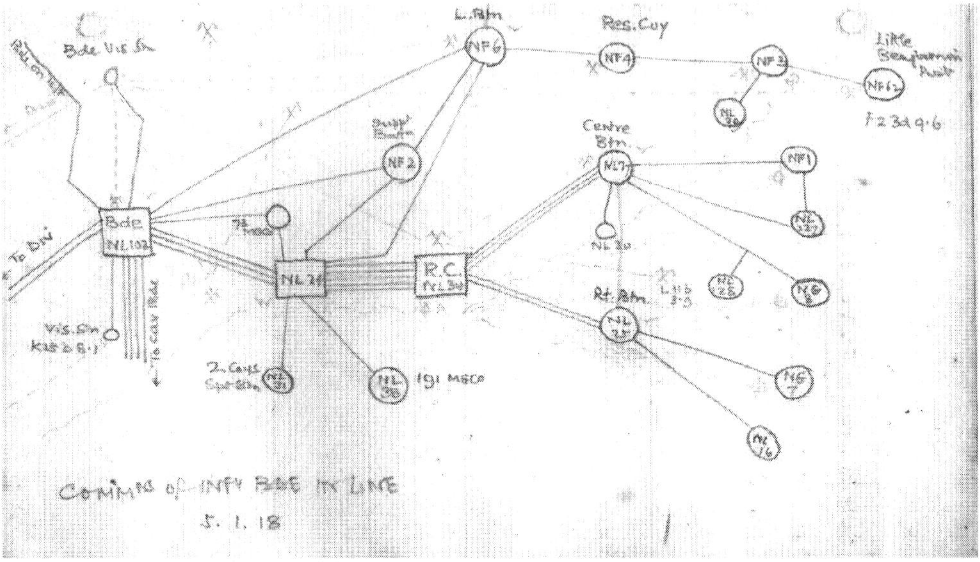
L. Btn
Res. Coy
Bde V.S. Stn
NF6
NF4
NF3
Centre Btn.
NF2
NF1
Bde
NL 102
To Div
NL 24
R.C.
Rt. Btn.
Vis. Stn
191 MGCo
To Cav Bde
COMMNS of INFY BDE IN LINE
5. 1. 18

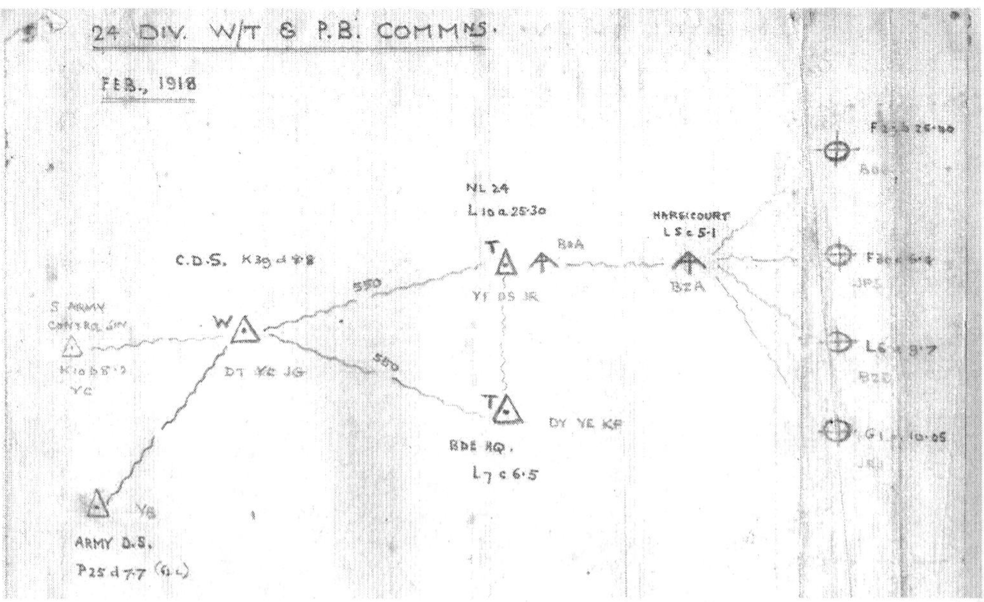
24 DIV. W/T & P.B. COMMNS.
FEB., 1918
NL 24
L 10 a. 25·30
HARSICOURT
L 5 c 5·1
C.D.S.
5 ARMY CONTROL STN
W
T
550
BZA
DT YE JG
DY YE KF
BDE HQ.
L 7 c 6·5
ARMY D.S.
P 25 d 7·7
L 6 a 9·7

I N S T R U C T I O N S "J". Aug '18

COMMUNICATIONS.

(a) Telephonic communications utilising Buried Cable Routes.

In the event of the BLACK or BROWN Line positions and O.Ps being occupied, the following arrangements have been made for the provision of commu nication t hrough the buried cable system, if this remains workable.

Signalling N.C.Os should be given the opportunity of acquainting themselves personally with the lines, test box locations, etc., in question.

To obtain communication on any of the lines given under "BROWN Positions" involving use of the Buried Routes, Brigade Signals would have to be informed in order that the necessary alterations and conn ections could be mad e.

BLACK LINE positions.

The O.Ps for the Black Line have been connected telephonically as follows:-

TOWER O.P. to A/106. Direct Line, Cable from O.P. to A 2 Test Box (M.11.b.9.6), thence by buried route to battery Signal Office.

JAMPOT O.P. to BDE.H.Q. Direct Line. Cable from O.P. to B Test Box (M.6.d.1.5.), thence by buried route and mine gallery cable to Bde. Signal Office.

SONIA O.P. to C/106. Cable from O.P. to B. Test Box (M.6.c.1.5) is joined to existing line from battery.

SONIA O.P. to C/106.(cont). to AURORA O.P. on the buried route.

JERRY O.P. to D/106. Cable from O.P. to A Test Box (M.11.a.7.1). is joined to existing line from battery to AURORA O.P. on buried route.

MOUND O.P. A cable runs from this O.P. to A 2 Test Box (M.11.b.9.6), and upon the O.P. becoming ready for use, this will be joined to the present D/106 - O.P. line.

In the event of the forward sections withdrawing to their batteries BROWN LINE positions whilst the batteries themselves are in their BLACK Line positions, communication could be got with BRIGADE H.Q. and through them to the batteries, by laying cable to the O.P.Exchange at R.11.a.8.5 as described below in para. 2 of "BROWN LINE communications".

BROWN LINE Positions.

On receipt of the order to "ManBattle Stations", there will be esta blished at different points in the Corps area, O.P. exchanges for the u se of Brig ades and Batteries, with a view to providing an immediate means of communication with one O.P. per Brigade for batteries on reaching their BROWN Line positions, pending the establishment of more complete communication.

INSTRUCTION "J". (cont)

The O. P. Exchange serving this brigade will be manned in these circumstances, at O D (formerly π D) Test Box at R.11.a.8.5., and will have communication to D.A., Brigade BROWN Line H.Q., Brigade Forward H.Q., and the BROWN Line O.P. at G.33.d.7.5., and also, as other lines become spare, with the O.P. at M.3.b.05.90.

Batteries can obtain communication with the O.P. exchange from their BROWN Line positions either by running cable direct, or by laying cable to O E (formerly π E) Test Box at R.12.a.25.70, and joining them there to existing cables running in a shallow open trench (caniveau), to the O.P. Exchange. At O E these terminate in a rack and are labelled for batteries of this Brigade. It is hoped shortly to substitute lines on the buried route for these cables

In tabulated form, therefore, the proposed communications for BROWN Line positions are as follows:-

<u>BDE. H.Q. and BTYS.</u> Between Rear H.Q. at R.12.a.70.52. and the ALOUETTES positions cable can be laid locally as circumstances permit.

Rear H.Q. will obtain communication with Forward H.Q. at MAROC through the O.P.Exchange.

<u>BDE. H.Q. and D.A.</u> Direct line on buried and mine gallery routes, with an alternative through the O.P.Exchange.

I N S T R U C T I O N "J". (cont)

<u>POMPEY O.P. to A/106.</u> If the buried route remains intact, Cable laid from the Battery BROWN position to FOSSE 11 or M.H. Test Box at M.9.c.0.2. would probably be an easier matter than to lay direct. In such a case a line should be laid from the O.P. to Test Box M.L.3. (formerly Box 12) at M.3.c.15.05., and joined to a lead which will be brought out of the box from a line on the bury running to M.H., or if required, FOSSE 11.

<u>NORTH POST O.P. to B/106.</u> A cable line run from the battery to O E Test Box above mentioned, and joined to No.2 cable on the caniveau route, will obtain communication with the O.P. Exchange, and through them, with the O.P.

<u>LONDON POST O.P. to C/106.</u> The nearest available point on the buried route to this O.P. is M P (formerly 16) Test Box at M.3.b.05.80. The line from O.P. of D/106 (M.3.b.05.90) to the O.P. Exchange runs through this box, as also lines to the Brigade. Forward H.Q. at MAROC. Visual is practicable from within the trench at the O.P. to the Brigade Visual O.P. at M.3.b.05.85.

Line No 5 from OE to the OP Exchange at OD on the caniveau route described above is available for C/106.

INSTRUCTION "J". (cont).

O.P. at M.3.b.05.90. to D/106.	From the battery to O.P.Exchange as for NORTH POST O.P. above, the cable being joined at O E to No. 3 on the caniveau. From the O.P., cable will be run to N P (formerly No.16) Test Box at M.3.b.05.80.

(b) Visual Communications.

Visual Communications in the Brigade area are as shewn on the accompanying diagram. In addition the Centre Infantry Brigade H.Q. is in visual communication with the Right and Left Battalions.

Batteries will ensure that the alignment of the stations with which they are in communication is familiar to their Signallers, so that visual communication may, if necessary, be resorted to without delay.

In the event of any lengthy failure of telephonic communication the visual stations of batteries (including the forward sections of C and D if still in their present positions), and that of Brigade H.Q. at M.3.a.0.0., will be manned automatically. In such a case inter-communication between Brigade H.Q. and C and D Btys would probably be more expeditious by runner direct.

On receipt of the order "Man Battle Stations" battery and brigade visual Stations will be manned, and in addition, the O.P. at M.3.b.05. 85. (Bde. Vis. Stn.), MOUND O.P. (or JERRY, if being used in place of MOUND), and JAMPOT O.P. will be manned for visual.

The O.P. at M.3.b.05.85. will be a combined visual Stn. and Group Rocket Stn.(see Instruction D).

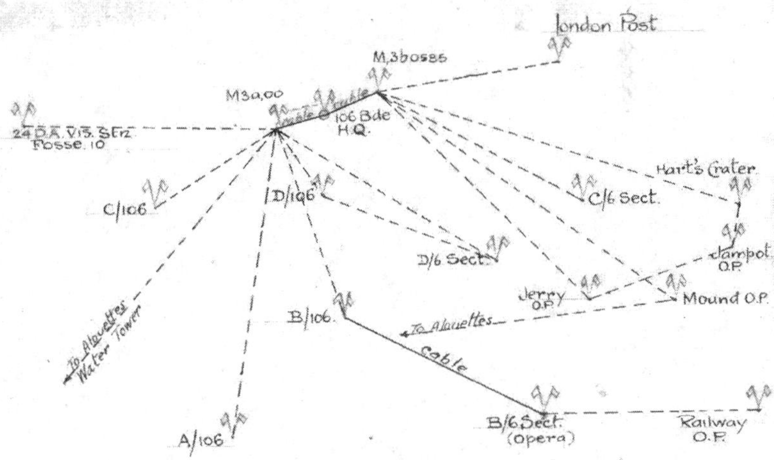

106 Bde. R.F.A.
Visual Communication

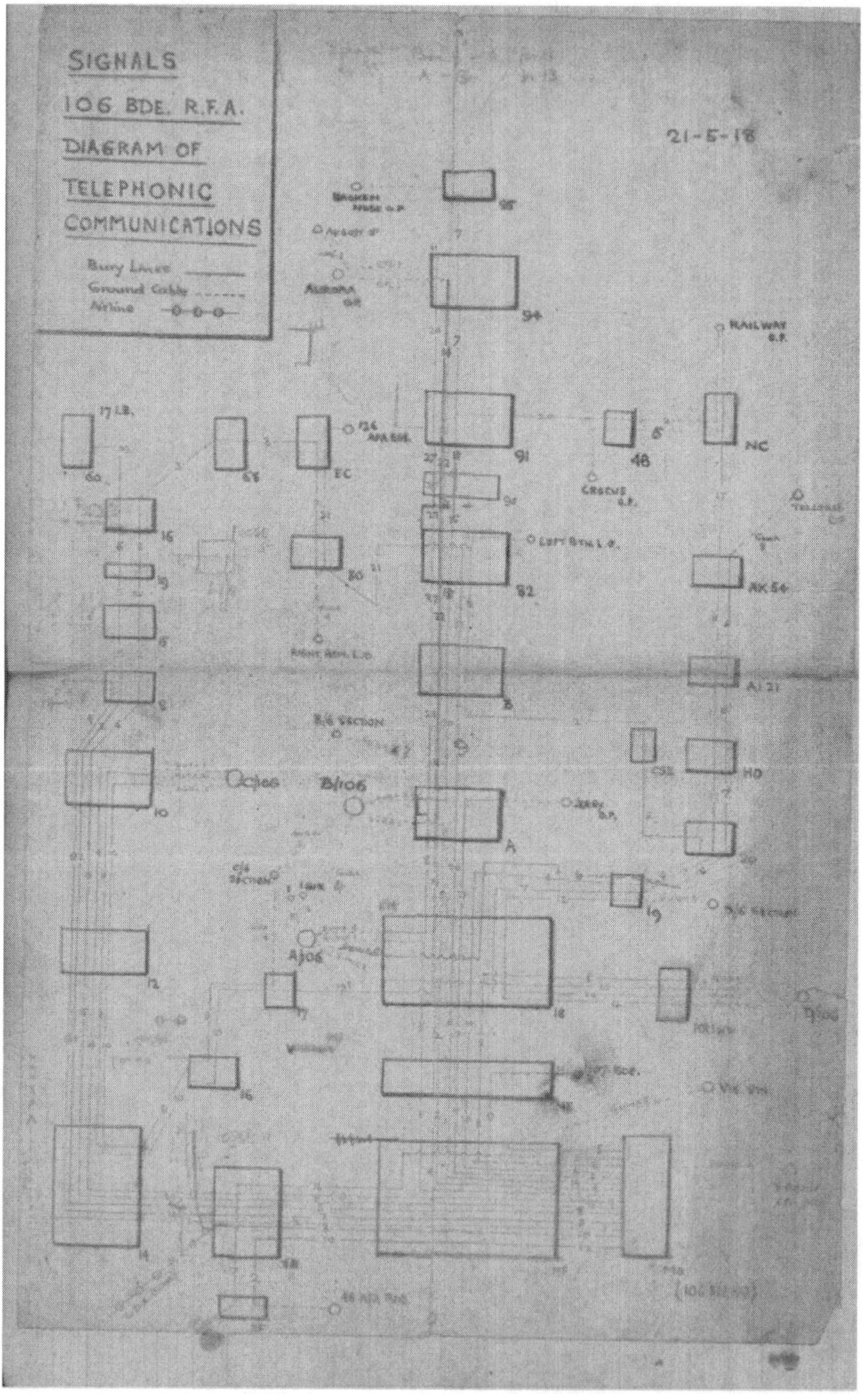
SIGNALS
106 BDE. R.F.A.
DIAGRAM OF
TELEPHONIC
COMMUNICATIONS
21-5-18
RAILWAY O.P.
AURORA O.P.
NC
48
91
94
82
AK 54
A1 21
HD
C/106
B/106
A/106
A
B/6 SECTION

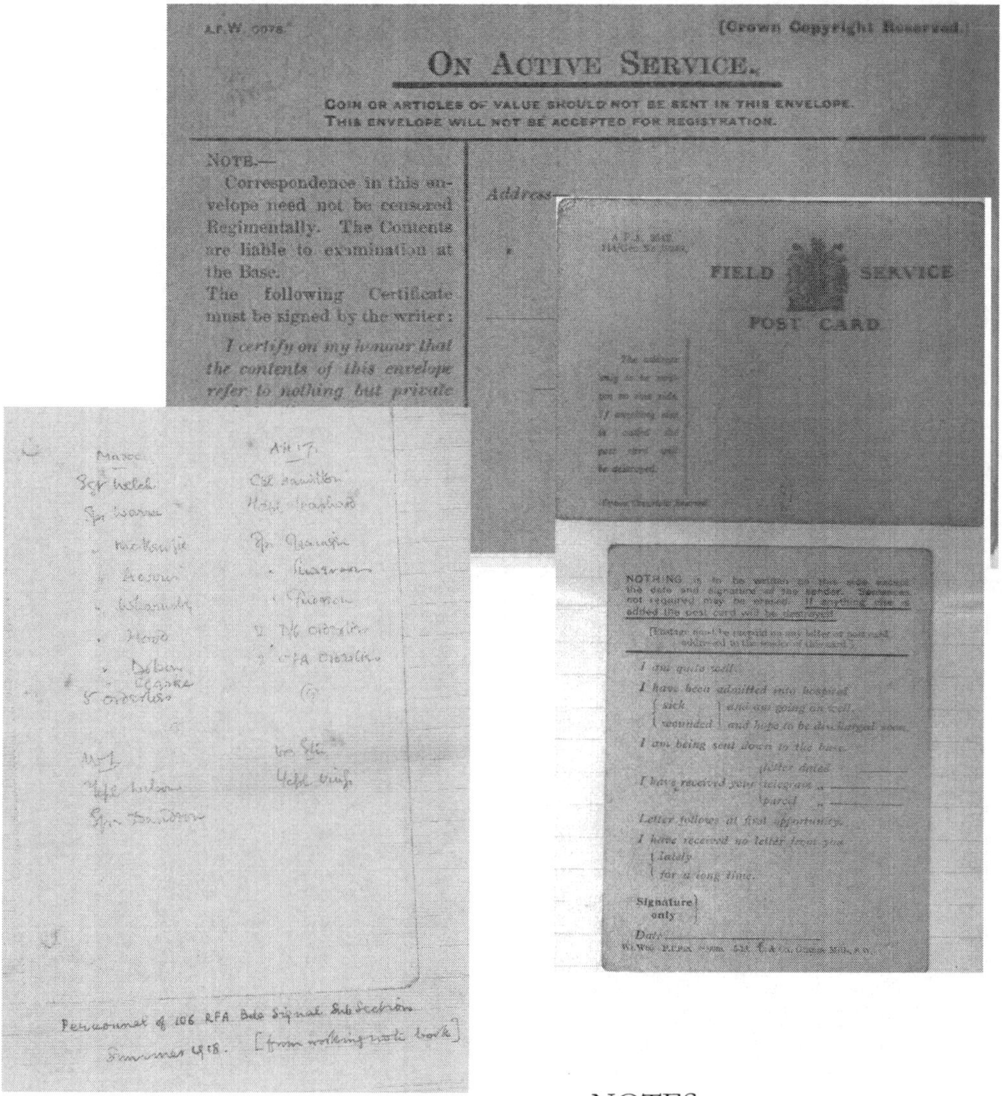

NOTES

Place names are those used at the time where these differ from those in use today.

Most of the abbreviations used by David will be self evident but for some I have either expanded the acronym or put a brief explanation in square brackets.